Salem
SOLDIER

Salem SOLDIER

**A journey from north Cardiganshire
to the ravages of war in north Africa and Italy**

Elfed & Brian Davies

To Lena, a wonderful wife and mother
And Nigel, a much loved son and brother

First impression: 2012

© Copyright Brian Davies and Y Lolfa Cyf., 2012

Cover design: Y Lolfa
Cover photograph: Brian Davies

ISBN: 978 184771 442 8

FSC

Published and printed in Wales
on paper from well maintained forests by
Y Lolfa Cyf., Talybont, Ceredigion SY24 5HE
website www.ylolfa.com
e-mail ylolfa@ylolfa.com
tel 01970 832 304
fax 832 782

Introduction

I NEEDED TO attend a meeting north of Machynlleth, so the offer of a day out was made to my father. The journey went well and it was decided to take a detour, leaving the main road which would have taken us through Bow Street. We travelled past Gogerddan to the now modern village of Penrhyn-coch, which has almost become a suburb of Aberystwyth. Entering what was once Penrhyn Isaf we continued past Pompren, Cwrt Farm and onto the ridge of Pen y Banc and to Bontgoch. Below, a view of our respective childhood valley, Penrhyn-coch, Salem and the streams of Silo and Stewi, triggered memories.

During the journey my father recalled needing to borrow a copy of *Old Moore's Almanack* before planning local concerts or eisteddfods in the old days, to find out the night of the full moon – a clear night would illuminate the journey for the participants and audience alike. The steep descent of the road into Talybont solicited another memory:

Mae'n hanner dydd cyn dyr y wawr, yng ngwaelod Cwm Eleri.
It's noon before dawn breaks in the depths of Cwm Eleri.

I suggested that these recollections should be recorded and shared, and some time later I was presented with a moving, detailed account of my father's early years. My own memories of a childhood within this caring community then came to mind. My father's formative years, his wartime separation from the community, his marriage and my own birth, and some of my own memories, have led to an appreciation of the significance of *cynefin* to the *Cymry cefn gwlad*.

Brian Davies
November 2012

CONTENTS

ELFED DAVIES

1919–2002

FATHER

1

Salem

I WAS BORN in September 1919, less than one year after the end of the First World War and in the opinion of many of my contemporaries a good few years too early. Nevertheless on reaching pension age and looking back one cannot but think, "If only I had..." However, one has to take many things such as circumstances etc. at the time, to assess of where one could have taken a slightly different path.

My place of birth and home was Salem, some six miles from Aberystwyth. A stone-built terrace house, two-up and two-down, with a coal shed behind and a privy, with a small garden adjoining it. As with almost every other house and cottage in the countryside in those days, it also had a pigsty nearby, with a *tomen* – a rubbish tip alongside this, because there was no refuse collection in rural areas. Every house burned coal for heating and cooking – so somewhere had to be found to tip the ashes also. These were mixed with all other household refuse (there was precious little tin food in those days), and was used as a compost or fertilizer for the garden in springtime. However, of the private houses in the village, we were the only one still rearing and killing a pig during my childhood.

We were a family of six girls and one boy. Up to the time I was about twelve years of age, my father was always working away in south Wales as a miner at Nant-y-Moel, as were very many men in the neighbourhood those days. There was very little work locally after the lead mines closed in the earlier part of the twentieth century. My father came home to see us every holiday, and regularly every Saturday morning the postman would bring a registered envelope with the housekeeping money for the week. Not a lot, but mother was a very good exchequer and budgeted for everything. Mother was the boss therefore and all decisions were hers. My eldest sisters Sal and Lizzie were soon working as servants; it was customary in those days. Sal was in service at a farm called Caergywydd near Bow Street, and Lizzie worked at the house of the tailors, Edwards of Penygroes, near Llandre. My other sister Glenys, after finishing Ardwyn School, also went into service temporarily at a house in Llandre while waiting to enter nursing. It was therefore quite an event for us younger ones, when the older girls walked over Banc-y-Cwrt to pay us a visit from time to time. Beattie, in due course, found work looking after children at a smallholding called Tyngwndwn near Cwmerfyn in the next valley. This left Hannah Mary and Megan, the youngest sister, at home with me. Hannah Mary won a scholarship to Ardwyn Grammar School. In those days entry was very limited and therefore competitive.

Salem hamlet is located just over a mile from Penrhyn-coch along a single-track road. When entering the village one comes across the Manse first. This was a large house belonging to the Congregational chapel in the village. It was a well-built double-fronted house, standing in its own grounds, a four-up and four-down, with a fireplace in every room, but not very modern by today's standard. There was also a purpose-built stable alongside the elevated garden, which had a loft to store fodder for the minister's horse.

Before I was a teenager, a man called Rev. Elias Jackson became our minister; we shared him with Siloah Chapel in Cwmerfin. He owned a small car – a Morris Cowley with a dickey seat behind; so the stable was altered to accommodate the car. In the Manse garden was the privy. However this one intrigued us children very much as it was a two-seater variety! This came to my mind many times in later years while abroad in the Army, where it was usual to have four- to six-seater versions!

Next along the village road was our house at the western end of a terrace of three. In fact it was officially called No.1 The Terrace, though almost everybody would call it (as was the habit then), Marged Ann's house – my mother's name. So familiar did the name become that in later years, twenty or thirty years after my mother's death, its then owners, who never knew her, put a nameplate on the door declaring it Marged Ann's. In those days the house did not have a back door, so everything had to be carried in through the front door including water, coal and refuse. There was an old-fashioned grate with a side oven and the usual collection of fire irons and a steel fender with a hob on either side. Below the fireplace was an ash pit with a grating to cover it, which had to be lifted every couple of days to clear the ashes away. The oven cooked fairly well, but it was often hit or miss; only my mother could make good use of it taking into account the type of coal to be used and direction of the wind etc.

At about eye level and at right angles to the fireplace was a bread baking oven which was very common in those days. This was brick-lined with an iron door – the smoke from it would enter the main chimney. It was heated with wood. Mother would make the dough for the bread and knead it in a large earthenware bowl. She would then put the dough into tins about twice the size of a large loaf today and lay them out on the fender, covered with a cloth to rise in front of the fire. The fire in the wall oven would be constantly checked and when all was well with just a few red charcoal embers glowing in the oven, the bread would go in, assisted by a long poker with a twist at the end to push the bread tins to the furthest corner. The oven door would be shut tight for the next couple of hours. The bread was enough to feed a family for a week. It was one of our rare treats to cut off a hot crust and have it with a lump of fresh butter.

All the villagers had to carry water from a well in the middle of the village and this continued until the mid 1930s when the council (using the same well) provided a pump alongside the road to make the task a little easier. Today the village has full mains supply water. One has to wonder how our home, like most others, managed to cook their meals at all on open fires with so few facilities, and I can't recall anyone being burned or scalded. In the early 1930s came a craze which was to revolutionize home cooking – the paraffin oil stove. Yet most households struggled to afford to buy one of these. The first and most popular one was a two-burner affair made by Valor. Improved models by Riffingiles and Florence were later made. When they were maintained in perfect condition, they were very good and a great boon to all households. Our first stove was a Valor but we later progressed to a Florence which remained in use until the 1950s when mother, one Saturday afternoon, misused it and almost burned the house down.

For home bread baking etc., my mother bought flour wholesale by the sack, but I doubt it would keep these days. When required she would purchase a sack-full during her shopping in the village, and it would be my job to borrow the shop's sack truck and wheel it through the village home: a pure white, coarse cotton sack with the lettering of Joseph Rank Flour Distillers printed on it. As we were the only home in the village still maintaining the old tradition, I felt very important entrusted to this task. The only other people still making bread at home were some of the surrounding farms.

Next door to our house lived a middle-aged bachelor Albert Williams with his aging mother, Liza Williams. When she died, he lived a meagre bachelor's existence with his undernourished dog. Albert also had a small triangular field on the way up to Penrhiw where he kept a few sheep, probably more for a hobby than profit. He had once worked in the lead mines and could be quite entertaining relating his experiences there. He also dabbled in writing poetry, and possessed a fine baritone voice which he exercised often.

The end terrace was occupied by Tom Edwards and his wife, Ann. They were both pensioners and their house was called Ann's House or Tŷ Ann. They were a very dear couple and great friends with all of us during our childhood – whenever we had any new clothing, Tom and Ann were always the first to see it. Tom's main hobby, apart from smoking his smelly Ringers Shag tobacco, was gardening and his pride and joy was his rhubarb. There weren't many motor cars on the road in those days, but there were still quite a few horses passing to and fro. Tom's favourite pastime was to watch at every opportunity to collect horse manure deposited on the roads and feed it to his precious rhubarb, and no doubt this paid off. As children would find it amusing to wager each other as to whether the latest visitors to Tŷ Ann, usually relations from Bow Street, would be given a bundle of rhubarb to take home.

Ann's hobby was housework and the whole house showed evidence of many years of wax polish (home-made of course) and elbow grease. Linoleum covered the floors in most houses in those days, as wall to wall carpeting was unheard of. In Ann's house, linoleum covered all the floors and the stairs as well. One amusing incident I remember: one morning, Ann rose first to prepare breakfast. It was customary in the country, especially during fine weather, for everybody to leave the front door wide open all day. Ann had already opened it on this particular morning. Tom came to the top of the stairs on his way down, wearing hand knitted socks, but he lost his footing and came down the highly polished stairs on his behind, just as on a bobsleigh in Switzerland. He came down at such a speed that he shot through the passage and found himself sitting in his stockinged feet in the middle of the road, vigorously protesting against Ann's wax polishing! Apart from his pride, thankfully he was not injured.

Apart from housework, Ann's other interest was St John's Church in Penrhyn-coch, where she was a staunch member – she was the only Church of England member living in Salem. She would attend morning service on Sundays, walking the mile and a half there and back. Tom and Ann were a very generous old couple and extremely hospitable. Nobody would come near their house without being offered tea and cakes etc.

Further along the village was another terrace of whitewashed cottages. Alongside the first one was an alley which was the entrance to the freshwater well which nearly all the villagers used. The first cottage was uninhabited at that time and was used as a storage place for its owner who lived next door in the middle cottage. His name was John David Rees, known to all as John Davy, a middle-aged bachelor who before the First World War had farmed Coedgruffydd, a local farm not that far from the village. He had sold out at an opportune time at the end of the war which had enabled him to take early retirement and enjoy a pleasant simple life.

He lived a fairly spartan existence – preparing his own food and doing housework, apart from clothes washing which was done for him by his next door neighbours. The floor of his living room and kitchen had bare blue flags and concrete, and he slept in the parlour. The kitchen had an indoor well to provide water for all his needs; in the living room was an old settle, some hard chairs, a grandfather clock and a fully dressed Welsh dresser.

He had, like all the other houses in the village, an old-fashioned fireplace with a side oven where he would cook his Sunday roast. We, like everyone else, were always made welcome when we popped in at any time – except Saturday afternoon, which was strictly laid aside for cottage cleaning and no one would be allowed to visit. The furniture would be polished and the floor washed. There would also be certain preparations made for Sunday, such as soaking a large basinful of dried peas, and, I would estimate, two packets of jelly in another large bowl. He would never eat all these himself and, more often than not, after we came home from school on a Monday, there would be a loud call of "ho-he-ho" from his doorstep and we would all race there to polish off the remains of the jelly and peas left over from Sunday.

He was an avid newspaper reader and he took at least two newspapers daily and some weeklies and was a keen student of current affairs. He also received a Welsh magazine called

Cymru'r Plant every month, and all the children of the village would gather at his house to read this.

Tŷ John Davy was also a sort of community centre for the whole village and many people would congregate there to yarn and debate the various burning topics of the day. When one would enter the living room (as no one would bother to knock), it would take a minute or two to identify who exactly was already present due to the thick fug of tobacco smoke! JD had also spent some time coalmining in the south – not for very long but long enough for him to store up endless stories which invariably started up with "There was a chap in Caerau etc. etc." Most of these stories were repeated many times and we knew them off by heart! His brother Ned still worked in Caerau and, after JD died in the 1950s, Ned retired and lived in his cottage in Salem but, though a most humorous character, he found life in Salem rather quiet. They were both laid to rest alongside each other in Salem cemetery.

As our father was away during most of our early years, we went to JD when we needed help to make a cart or fix a wheel on some toy. He had a good selection of hand tools, saws, brace, bits, planes etc. Though we were never allowed to handle these for safety reasons, he brought them out for any job, sometimes after a bit of pestering and cajoling on our part. He was a man of great patience. He had one great theory that whatever he bought – be it tools or a new pair of boots – they had to be the very best available and he looked after them accordingly. Another job he undertook during my childhood was cutting hair, that is, the boys at least, and probably a few other adult residents of the time too. This was always performed with great gusto which would account for the difficulty my mother had in catching me and forcing me to attend the ritual!

Next door to JD lived my favourite playmate, Ifor James, with his parents and grandmother. He was a year older than me and as we were the only two boys in the village, we were very close playmates. Their house was unusual as it only had a half-loft over a parlour, with stairs going up from the living room. Over the fireplace was a huge mantle and we would sit under this round the fire. This, no doubt, was a relic of the old fire on the floor that was popular before grates and fireplaces came along.

Next along the road was a house standing in its own grounds, Arosfa, and it had fairly recently been renovated but not modernized. An old couple lived there during my childhood, then when the Rev. Jackson came to live in the manse, the temporary residents of the manse, Robert Edwards and his wife, moved to live in Arosfa, together with their son Owen Penry. They lived there until the 1950s. (After marriage Owen Penry lived in Penrhyn-coch for years.) Mr and Mrs Edwards hailed from the Tywyn area originally but had settled down to life in Salem, with their main interest being singing in the chapel.

Across the road was the chapel cemetery with its surrounding wall, yew trees and double iron gates at the top of a fairly steep path leading down to the chapel door. Next to the cemetery, but below the level of the road, was a house called Tan y Ffordd; it was steeped in Salem's history and the Joneses lived there for generations. During my childhood Tan y Ffordd was occupied by George Harvey, his wife and daughters. To us George was a most amusing and entertaining character who taught us to do all kinds of tricks. An Englishman, he had come from an orphanage to work in the area. He now worked doing odd jobs for a Mrs Smith, who lived further along the village. He taught us how to make whistles from sycamore trees, how to play a mouth organ, how to make a crude one-string instrument. To us children, George could do no wrong.

Below the road and in front of Tan y Ffordd was another well, used mainly by the residents of that end of the village and also the horses belonging to the shop – another excellent supply of pure water that had stood the test of time and had never been known to run dry. At the far end of the cemetery wall and across the road was a fairly steep lane leading up to Penrhiw. This was another hamlet of some eight to ten houses, built alongside the road that ran up to the lakes and the mountain. The road through Salem, however, continued on to Coedgruffydd Farm.

Nearby was a small purpose-built village shop with an adjoining warehouse. The proprietors of this shop, Gwilym Lewis and his wife and daughter, also farmed the surrounding land. Gwilym's father had been the shopkeeper cum farmer before him. The shop provided for the needs for almost all the residents, some of which were quite large families. Not only provisions but also, very importantly, the paraffin to light homes and use for cooking, as there was no electricity at that time in the 1920s. Bottle gas had not been heard of then. The shop also supplied flour for baking bread, and animal and chicken feedstuff. The warehouse was located opposite the cemetery gates. Alongside also were a cowshed and a cart house, another popular place for children to rendezvous during rainy weather. Next, past the shop, were two single-storey cottages which were used as a stable and storehouse. The stable housed two shire mares named Brown and Star, together with all their harness.

There was always a great excitement amongst us children when the big (to us then) lorries came to deliver supplies to the shop. As the years went by the lorries grew bigger and alterations had to be made to the shop corner for the lorries to be able to turn around. We always took a lot of interest in the shop and farm, no more so than when Gwilym had to deliver a few bags of animal feed to various farms in the horse and cart, and we accompanied him to help open the gates.

Further past the shop was Mrs Smith's bungalow – then a construction of asbestos and wood almost buried behind a thick hedge. She was an Englishwoman who had earlier farmed Coedgruffydd before retiring to the bungalow and letting her son Bryan carry on. She also owned the terrace of houses where we lived and we paid rent to her. She was a founder member of Salem Women's Institute, and was the first person in the area to have a telephone.

There was one further cottage near the bungalow before

the lane dipped down to Coedgruffydd Farm itself. We called this stone cottage Bancyn Bach and it was occupied by yet another member of the Jones clan. During the early part of the First World War, English immigrants took it over, and lived there for many years. The stable cottages were also completely refurbished to make a very comfortable bungalow at this time too. It remained like this until the 1960s when it was completely demolished and a modern bungalow built instead.

Several people tried to make a living from the shop, but eventually it closed. The shop was modernized to make the comfortable dwelling which stands there today. Coedgruffydd Farm itself was split up amongst other farms.

Some 100 yards up Penrhiw Lane from the shop corner stood another neat cottage with a nice front garden, by the name of Gwargerddi. As the name describes, the cottage was built out of line with the other roadside dwellings and behind the gardens. In those days Margaret Jones, an aged spinster, lived at Gwargerddi. She was well into her 80s and lived with her niece, Margaret Ann, who cared for her and supplemented their meagre pension with a little sewing and quilting. There was another member of the family too, in the form of Thomas the cat, or more correctly a huge tomcat, slate coloured and known to all of us children as Thomas Gwargerddi. It was easy to deduce from his appearance that old Thomas enjoyed a very good life.

Quite a number of visitors, relatives etc. from the south would always be staying at Gwargerddi during the summer months. And when the chapel did not have its own minister, the visiting preacher would also be lodging there and without doubt would have had a great welcome.

We children had certain regular duties expected of us each evening after school and also on Saturday: a message for this, and a message for another. One of the most regular chores was to fetch the milk for Gwargerddi from Brogynin down the lane. We would carry the milk in wine or a similar sort of corked bottle, in a straw shopping bag. These chores often impaired on our play but there was compensation in the form of a penny or a bright red apple which grew in profusion in the garden below the house.

If the weather was unsuitable for playing outside afterwards, we would sit on the fender by the feet of the old lady with Thomas, the tomcat, sleeping peacefully as usual on the rag mat in front of the fire. With her eyes tightly closed old Margaret Jones would relate to us what life was like when she was our age.

Just like most other men in the community during her childhood, her father was a miner and we would be astounded to hear that she also as a twelve-year-old had to go down the mine to work at Lletty Ifan Hen. Her first job was to hold a candle to enable her father to drill the rock for blasting. We were shocked to learn of the small wage for this work, bearing in mind that each miner had to buy his own candles and black powder for blasting. And all this whilst constantly wet to the skin – in winter the miner's clothes would be frozen to his body before he would finish the long walk home.

A story of great interest to us was how Gwargerddi came to be built in its location. Her father, despite his meagre earnings, was anxious to build a new house for his family and for this purpose he'd already collected suitable stone from the surrounding banks and fields. There was no such thing as planning permission in those days. The only thing impairing his dream was a lack of suitable building plot. In those days Salem and the surrounding area was part of the Brogynin Estate and owned by Squire Richards who lived in Plas. It was customary for the squire to do his rounds of the estate on horseback, through Salem village, down to Coedgruffydd and circle back to Brogynin. He expected every man he saw to raise his cap to him, and each woman to curtsey. However, Margaret Jones's father decided he would never doff his cap to anyone, ever. This minor rebellion had gone on for years – when the time came for him to go to the squire to buy a plot of land next to the road to build a house, it was the turn of the squire to be stubborn! The bargaining went on for quite some time. However, a compromise was eventually reached – the squire would sell a plot to him, but not along the road but behind the gardens on the lane leading to Penrhiw. The reason – so that when the squire came by, he would not be able to see John Jones not doffing his hat to him. So, the cottage was built and very aptly named Gwargerddi, meaning above the gardens. It was a comfortable home for many generations and despite numerous changes of ownership in recent years, the old name has been retained which is such an integral part of the history of the village.

2

A Mystery

IN THE LATE 1920s, when I was about eight or nine years old, something happened which has remained very vividly in my memory ever since. I was at living with my mother and three sisters and attending school at Trefeurig at the time. Every morning I'd walk to Penrhiw, meet children who lived there and a hamlet called Llwynprysg. We'd all walk down in a group on a rough track through Banc Tyngelli towards the school, while at the same time watch other children across the valley doing the same thing from the direction of Banc y Daren. We'd all eventually meet up by the river bridge before walking the last twenty yards to school. This would be the regular pattern every day whatever the weather. Penrhiw was at high elevation and very exposed, so much so that the older children had to hold on to the youngsters so that they didn't blow away. The Parish Council had erected a wicket gate instead of a farm gate to enter the rough track of Banc Tyngelli, as even the older ones could not manage the large gate in the high wind. Of course, there was no such thing as a ride to school in those days!

Some half a mile from Salem lies the three Brogynins, a famous name in Welsh history – allegedly the birthplace of the famous bard Dafydd ap Gwilym. One was called Brogynin Fawr, and the occupants were a middle-aged couple called Barsilai Jones and his wife Mary. He led the singing in the chapel, with his wife playing the organ. The other was Brogynin Fach; it was farmed by the Hugheses. Plas Brogynin was a large house where, as mentioned earlier, the squire once lived. But, during my childhood the large house was split in two. The rear part was occupied by a middle-aged couple called John and Sue Jones. I vividly recollect that their yard was always very muddy! The front part of the house was the home of a retired widowed Methodist minister, his daughter Dilys and an elderly housekeeper. Now Miss Dilys Jones was my class teacher at Trefeurig School, a charming young lady about 30 years of age and worshipped by all the children. She owned a little car and there were very few who could say that at that time. She would use the car to ferry her father to various preaching engagements on a Sunday and to their chapel at Capel Dewi. She never used the car to go to work at Trefeurig School every day; she preferred to walk over Penrhiw with us children in tow, a bit like the Pied Piper. She seemed to enjoy this, as did the rest of us.

One summer, we'd been to school as usual on the Monday with Miss Jones as our escort. On Tuesday morning, before we were up, there was heavy knocking on our door. John Jones from Plas Brogynin was there asking my mother to go with him – Miss Jones was very ill. My mother went of course, leaving us to get up and prepare for school. However, before we left for school, having made some sort of scratch breakfast for ourselves, mother returned carrying a newborn baby in a blanket in her arms, and telling us that our beloved Miss Jones was dead after giving birth to a little girl. Nobody had known that she was with child.

One can only imagine the shock to her aged father and housekeeper. Mother, however, in her usual practical manner stepped in and found our old crib, or as she would say Cader. She rummaged around for various items to try and clothe the little baby. In those days there was no district nurse to call upon and rural areas relied on people like my mother. But in this instance there had been no preparation at all. The news spread like wildfire and we made our way to school on our own. I will never forget that morning. At Trefeurig School we had a headmaster, Dan Jones, an infants' teacher called Miss Edwards and Miss Jones. All the children were crying uncontrollably and so were the teachers. After a short while we were all sent home, much to our relief. We could now go home to see the new baby.

Mother, true to her nature, had things organized and pretty soon the little one was thriving. Her grandfather and housekeeper would visit her every day and soon gave her the name Margaret. But little Margaret was also an embarrassment to the minister, as she was being looked after by a local woman in the village. So, after discussing this with mother, it was agreed that they would attempt to bring the baby up themselves.

Arrangements were made whereby they would come to our house every morning to see to the needs of Margaret, bathing and feeding etc. After about a week's instruction, the minister and housekeeper felt confident that they could cope and so, much to our regret, the little one was returned home to Plas Brogynin to be brought up by her grandfather and his housekeeper.

Our home reverted to normal, but not for long. During the first night, in the early hours, there was another loud knock on our door and once again it was John Jones begging my mother to come again. Little Margaret had shown them who was the boss and they were forced to getting more help from my mother. I recall mother returning in the early morning carrying the little one once again in a blanket, to be placed back in the crib with the fire stoked up to keep her warm. She remained with us for a few more weeks and, by this time, the old minister had made arrangements for her to be adopted by someone from Llangurig.

None of us saw Margaret again but mother said that a few years later, while walking the promenade at Aberystwyth on a bank holiday, someone did point her out playing on the beach. My mother died in 1960 but during the 1970s I learned that Margaret was now the conductor of a Llangurig choir. Her marital status was not known. She died in the early 1980s. We will never know if she learned the true story of her early childhood or the identity of her father.

3

Transport and Modernization

BEFORE THE 1920s, in the absence of motor traffic, country roads weren't tarred and metalled – they were all rough and unmade. In the summer dry weather, therefore, motor traffic such as there was, was always followed by a large cloud of white dust which would settle on hedges and adjoining fields. Therefore, in the late 1920s, a big campaign was launched to have all the minor roads through the small villages tarred – that is, the part of the road where it entered the village to its exit at the other end, just to alleviate the nuisance of the dust entering houses and settling on gardens. This was doubly important in this part of the county as we all realized that much of the road-making material used on these roads would come from the lead mine spoil heaps nearby, such as Cwmswmlog and Cwmerfyn which have now thankfully disappeared.

These would have contained an unknown quantity of poisonous slurry from the mine washeries, such as lead, which flying about in summer was a great hazard to all. The County Council finally agreed to tar each road through a village, leaving only the roads in between rough. It was custom in those days for farmers to gather stones from hayfields in the spring, and deposit them in a cairn at some convenient spot alongside the roads for later use by road repairers. This is mentioned in Tom MacDonald's book *The White Lanes of Summer*; collecting stones was another way for us children to make a penny or two if we were lucky enough to find a generous farmer.

I have mentioned the small amount of motor traffic. However, there was a very enterprising individual by the name of John Morgan, Brynhyfryd (which lies between Salem and Penrhyn-coch). He started a motor bus service between Salem and Aberystwyth every Monday (market day) at 10 a.m. and 1 p.m. returning at 4 p.m. and 7 p.m. (After the Second World War the last bus service returned at 5.30 p.m., as the shops were now closing earlier.) There were exceptions to these times, in particular during the three-week hiring fairs in November. At first John Morgan owned an old Ford T, a very adaptable vehicle, since on Tuesday mornings parts of the bodywork, together with most of the seats, would be removed and it would now be converted to a coal lorry! John Morgan and his son John James had another enterprise in those days too – he also ran a motor taxi service with an American Overland car.

Before the motor bus service started a horse-drawn brake took passengers to and from town, run by John Magor who lived at Penyberth, Penrhyn-coch. This service continued until the competition grew too strong and he gave up, bringing the era of horse transport to an end.

One night, however, in the winter of 1922 a catastrophe occurred in the bus and taxi garage: the building burnt to the ground. From all accounts nothing was insured, so John Morgan had to start again. He managed to rebuild his garage himself and bought a twenty-seater Fiat bus. This became popular, as did the cinemas in town on a Saturday evening. So, the bus service was extended to departing at 4.00 p.m. on Saturday and returning 8.30 p.m. There was much speculation as to what the latest epic to watch would be. Aberystwyth boasted three good cinemas at this time. The Coliseum was converted from a purpose-built old music hall and it still stands – it's now the county museum. The Pier Pavilion and the Celtic were converted from old swimming baths after their predecessor, the Palladium, burnt down.

Children were hardly ever allowed to go to the pictures, probably due to the cost. The price of admission was anything between 1s 3d to 2s 3d or maybe 2s 9d, that's 6p to 13p in today's money. The return bus fare was 1s 9d.

Later, a Thursday service was also introduced to cater for the midweek shows.

The bus, as mentioned, was supposed to be a twenty-seater but that was of no importance at all, especially on the return journey. What governed capacity (note, not the seating capacity) was how many could be packed in, sitting or standing! Sardines in a tin were nothing to this! The bus's poor springs would be groaning as each corner was taken. However, this old bus and subsequent buses with severe overloading didn't suffer a single accident and it was a very rare occurrence for the bus to break down.

There were, in those days, some very regular passengers on the Monday service. Previously mentioned John Davy Rees was one, and another was Richard Edwards, Clawddmelyn, a farm outside Salem. He was totally blind, but would take a large basket of eggs and butter to sell in town every Monday, and would do all his shopping and also shopping for anyone else in the village before returning home. It was assumed by everybody that his uncanny way of making his way between shops in town was due to his keen sense of smell, and with more shops opening their doors throughout the day; it was even easier to smell a chemist, a shoe shop or a grocer and make your way around. What used to amuse us children when the bus came to the end of its journey in Salem was that John Morgan would have to wake up Richard. Richard would have nodded off at the rear of the bus, despite the jolts of the rough Salem road.

At the end of Second World War a daily bus service to town was established, partly because the local education authority had contracted bus operators to carry children to secondary school. This revolutionized bus operators, especially the small operator. However this came a good few years too late for me to

take advantage of it, so I never went any further than Trefeurig
Primary School.

My older sisters, Lizzie, Glenys and Hannah Mary all passed
the scholarship entrance exam as it was known then (later
known as the 11+). Arrangements were made for each one of
them to lodge with an aunt in Aberystwyth because of the lack
of a daily bus service at the time. Lizzie did not stay very long
in secondary school but both Glenys and Hannah Mary stayed
on to take their exams. As for me, although I was considered
fairly bright at Trefeurig School, by the time I was due to start
studying the scholarship exam, the Great Depression had
arrived and with my father now on the dole, it was obvious
that my parents could not afford letting me stay on at school.
I remember my old schoolmaster, Dan Jones, coming over one
evening to try to persuade my mother to influence me to sit
the entrance exam, but to no avail – my mind was made up.
Thinking back, it wouldn't have made much difference anyway
financially, as the first job I had on leaving school at 14 only
paid 5s a week, which went to pay for lodging in Aberystwyth.
The main difference probably, as my mother had learned from
experience, was that to be in secondary school in those days
incurred a lot of other expenses, such as paying for books,
clothes, equipment etc. I deeply regretted not having had the
chance though, and I feel sure that I could have succeeded, but
the lack of transport and inconvenience put a stop to it and
cycling the six miles of hills to school in all weathers was not
my cup of tea.

I was not the only one who didn't go to secondary school
– few of my age who lived in the upper part of the valley
managed to get any secondary education at all. But, lower
down the valley, in Penrhyn-coch, things were rather different
and quite a few of my contemporaries managed to carry on
with their education. This was not a reflection of ability, but
more of geography.

Deep down I felt frustrated about this, so much so that I
pleaded to be allowed to join one of the armed services as a boy

apprentice, but of course my mother soon put the damper on any such ideas. Looking back and having done six and a half years in the Army a few years later, would it have been *such* a bad idea?

However, at the time I showed great interest in carpentry and did quite a lot of fretwork in the evening at home. Little good light, other than the oil lamp, was the main drawback but I continued and even saved my pocket money and, when Woolworths came to Aberystwyth, I managed to buy a few odd tools such as a saw, drill, hammer etc. at sixpence each. I still possess some of these. But my ambition to be a carpenter was cut short very early, when someone told me that every carpenter would be required to make coffins and that they would have to put dead bodies in them. That did it – the end of my carpenter's ambition!

4

Country Life

THERE WERE A number of ways to amuse ourselves in my youth. We had a keen interest in sheep and during harvest time we would probably try to help in some way. Farm work was much more labour intensive then than it is today (now almost one man can complete the harvest on his own with modern machinery and equipment). Not so then when every farm, large or small, had to rely on help to complete the task. The custom those days was that anyone could plant a row of potatoes in the local farmer's field, which would then grow and be harvested at the same time as the farmer's own crop. This would give villagers a good stock of potatoes to keep them going throughout the winter. In recompense it was expected that help would be given during the harvest, the hay and corn harvest as well. This sort of arrangement was carried out for many years, and even when we set up home in Penrhyn-coch after the war, we still helped out at busy times during the 1950s at Coedgruffyd Farm. But, by this time tractors had taken the place of the horses – which made a great difference.

Mother was quite a dressmaker. She owned an old Singer sewing machine and made very good use of it. There were many hand-me-downs through the use of the Singer and their useful life was considerably extended, much to the benefit of the youngsters in the family. When my sisters, for instance, went into domestic service, my mother would invariably provide them with an adequate supply of aprons, made from material she would have bought at a bargain price at the November fairs in Aberystwyth.

She would make clothes from flour sacks. These were made from good coarse, cotton material, pure white apart the name stencilled red on them. This, with a slight bleaching, would almost disappear, but not quite.

Another one of my mother's hobbies was wallpapering and she was very capable and therefore in some demand with neighbours, family and friends. She also had a keen interest in an old quack remedy recipe for the cure of shingles handed down to her. After hearing that someone in the neighbourhood was suffering from the complaint, she would send me out to Pen Gaer nearby to pick a bunch of green leaves which grew in profusion there in the stone hedge bank. She would mash these to a pulp with a hammer on a chopping board and then mix them with some melted lard in a saucepan, and when cooled, she would strain through muslin. The result was a green-coloured ointment which she would put in a jar and send to the person suffering. From all reports this never failed and my greatest regret is the fact that I have forgotten which leaf it was, much to my dismay.

I can remember my sister Glenys leaving home at 18 to train as a nurse at the Manor Hospital in Walsall. She wrote home every week. Mother took great interest in the letters and no less so when Glenys described in one how they had a female patient on her ward who was suffering terribly with shingles, despite every effort of the doctors to cure her. Glenys knew all along that her mother had a cure, but said nothing. However, she could stand the suffering of this woman no longer, and eventually wrote to mother. I was dispatched at once to Pen Gaer for a supply of leaves and by post the same evening, the ointment was on its way. Glenys was on night duty and told the patient about her mother's ointment. She readily agreed to try the ointment without the knowledge of anyone else at the hospital. The woman was immediately cured.

As children we would play at Penrhiw on Banc Tyngelli and would be joined by children from Penrhiw and Llwynprisg and also quite a number of English children who occupied the summer houses in the village during the holidays. Penrhiw was a good place to view all the activities that went on. In those days it was usual to see at least one warship visiting the bay just off Aberystwyth beach each summer. This was quite a tourist attraction and would help the local boatmen make a few extra pounds by ferrying sightseers. The evening attraction was the warship's searchlight display. This would happen most evenings after dark and would light up the sky and distant hills around the bay. It was a magical display, but little did we realize that in a few short years that sight would strike terror in us as we realized that the enemy was in the sky and that the lights were searching for it.

My friend Ifor and I took a great interest in water divining at that time too, with the aid of a hazel fork held in our hands in a certain way. We would walk around for miles practising this and, even to this day, I can remember exactly where the best contacts were found. We also discovered that the same method could be used to find certain lead veins that were near the surface in surrounding fields. Once found we would check our findings with John Davy Rees. He'd bring out the mineral maps of the surrounding area which he'd had since his farming days. We learned, with lots of practice, how to differentiate between water and other mineral contact, and we were able to gauge the depths etc. At the end of the war the shop and farm were now under new owners. To prove the accuracy of our findings it appears that the new owner had sunk a well to water his cattle at the very spot we'd found this spring many years before. So much for the scientists on TV who claim these days that divining is old wives tales and mumbo jumbo!

There was no electricity in the country areas in those days, and we thought little about how its advent would make life easier for us in the future for instance. The chapel at Salem was cleaned and cared for by my mother for almost forty years. Not just cleaning and dusting either, because there was lighting and heating to take care of too. There were twelve oil lamps, with most suspended from the high ceiling and also a couple of paraffin oil heating stoves. All these had to be maintained regularly. Oil was carried to them, wicks trimmed, glasses cleaned and even then it was rather poor light. When there was a special midweek event, such as a thanksgiving service or a choir practice etc., the ritual of preparing the lights had to be faced. All activities took place in the chapel (as there was no vestry or hall at that time) or else at Trefeurig schoolroom in the next valley. As with most organizations then events were arranged to raise funds for maintenance. Chapels and churches would hold concerts, dramas, eisteddfodau etc., all with varying degrees of success, depending on the effort put into it. In Salem there were eisteddfodau, grand concerts, social evenings with tea and a gossip and various raffles. I understand that this is carried on to this day, though now held in the village hall at Penrhyn-coch since the 1950s.

The eisteddfod and concerts meant a lot of work when they were held in the chapel, such as erecting a purpose-made stage in the *set fawr* or elders' pew. Hiring or borrowing a pick-up, transporting the stage with much difficulty to the chapel, and making sure it was on time. I can remember some excellent concerts held there with some of Wales's top artists of the day taking part. In the absence of TV and radio, it was wonderful entertainment and included singers, harpists, choirs etc.

An easier way to raise funds was the social evening, comparable with today's coffee morning. But, in Salem in those years, there was a snag; whereas we were able to sit quite a number in the middle of the chapel floor and prepare the food in the side pews all around, the biggest problem was boiling the water. Not to be deterred, a few volunteers built a small 6' x 6' corrugated zinc shed in the corner of the cemetery near the chapel's back door. Here we had a large cast-iron urn with a tap, mounted on a trivet. A fire heated the water and the smoke escaped through a chimney. Wonderful idea, except that since the shed and its chimney was so near to the chapel building, it was almost impossible to get the chimney to draw. The result was a shed-full of smoke and whoever was nominated the job

35

of stoker and water boiler for the evening, if he wasn't an ex-coalminer before the event, he certainly looked like one after the night was over! No wonder then that the job fell to my father more often than not. What we could have done with Calor Gas in those days...!

Other villages had functions to contribute to the fund too. Bontgoch, for instance, had an annual eisteddfod, so too did Madog and also Horeb, Penrhyn-coch. But in the early 1930s, a purpose-built vestry was built at Penrhyn-coch which solved most of their problems and is in constant use today.

Oil lamps were still with us though until the 1950s, when the electricity supply was extended to all country areas and was a great boon to all. Some functions were held then at Trefeurig Primary School, and there was a lot of work involved in preparing the hall (which consisted of two classrooms divided by a folding partition and a portable stage erected at one end). Most concerts, choir practices, Parish Council meetings, elections were held here, as well as the school's Christmas concert with the inevitable Christmas tree and a visit from Santa Claus. I can well remember one Christmas when we produced our own pantomime, *Dick Whittington*, and I was Dick and my sister Megan the suitably dressed cat, which brought the house down. However, by the time next Christmas came around, Megan had a badly infected knee joint which she had to have removed and she lay in a hospital in Denbigh, some 80 miles away. At that year's Christmas concert, old Tommy Morgan, Cartrefle stood up and said that they all had her in their thoughts that night. A collection hat went round and the monies was handed to my mother; there were enough pounds to pay for a taxi to visit Megan in hospital.

The school played a very important part in our lives in those days: you could stand on Penrhiw almost any night and look down towards the school and there was always a light on with something or other going on. We must bear in mind is that there was no TV or radio in those days, so we had to provide all entertainment ourselves. Another great contrast to today was that everybody walked everywhere to whatever was going on: concerts, whist drives, dramas or whatever, perhaps with the help of a torch.

Torches make me recall an old story from the 1920s of an old couple called Dafydd and Mary Ann, Lluestfach, who ran a sheep-farming small-holding up in the mountains near Cwmsymlog. They had come down to Cwmsymlog village one afternoon to visit, intending to return to their house before dark. However, night fell before they were able to leave, so some kind person in the village lent them a torch. Normally they would have brought their lantern with them if they had intended to stay late. However, on reaching home with the torch, they wondered how to put it out. Both of them had a go at blowing it out, but to no avail. So they found the bellows – used in those days to help get the fire going. They had another go at blowing out the torch, and encouraged each other by saying that they thought they were winning as the light grew dimmer, not realizing of course that the battery was becoming exhausted! When it came time to go to bed, they put the torch in a bucket of water to make sure the house wouldn't burn down whilst they slept. Needless to say this action was successful in putting the light out!

I can remember our neighbour, Albert Williams, telling us that when he was younger he had a mining job in Pontrhydygroes. There was no transport to get him there – so every Monday morning meant a very rough cross-country walk of at least ten to twelve miles; he'd stay there during the week and make the return journey on Friday or Saturday. He would relate many stories about the Camdwr and Bwlchglas mines high up in the hills to the east of Bontgoch. The mining companies at Cwmdwr had built barracks to house the workers. But these were very primitive, with no facilities for cooking and drying wet clothes etc. My father also worked under those conditions, as did most men in those days. If you walk through the cemeteries of the area today and read the inscriptions on the tombstones, you realize that when a miner died at the age of 40, it would have been considered a good innings. Yes, life in the generation preceding mine was very hard.

My youngest sister, Megan, was born on 28 December 1921. Our father was at home at the time from south Wales. He had to move pretty fast during the night to fetch the nurse and midwife. This meant a walk in the dark, with a lantern in his hand, past Tynpynfarch over Banc y Cwrt, down to Rhydypennau to Bronceiro to fetch Nurse Rees, daughter of J T Rees the famous musician. She, in turn, would have to call her brother, Goronwy Rees, to drive the pony and trap up to Salem – my father with his lantern in the trap, and all having to walk up the steep hill past Horeb chapel. Nurse Rees had to do the journey herself for the next ten days on her bicycle as my father had returned to south Wales by now, with my aunt from near Capel Madog coming to stay and watch after us all.

In those days it was easy to identify all the miners coming and going to south Wales by their luggage. There were no suitcases then, but a straw basket with a strong leather strap to hold it together. There'd be the inevitable label with the owner's name on it, declaring also the destination of the passenger. Firstly there would be the walk to the station to catch the train at Aberystwyth (as there weren't many buses and none convenient for the train). And life would, once again, return to waiting for the morning post and the registered letters that would bring us our meagre existence.

The post in those days was surprisingly reliable. The post for the whole area would be dropped off in Bow Street and Richard Thomas would start his long hike with a full bag of mail, to be met at Penrhyn-coch post-office by two part-time postmen. One would do his round covering Cefnllwyd and adjoining farms, the other in the direction of Tynpynfarch and the other farms. Dick the Post, as he was popularly known, would go on to Salem where he would meet again with a part-timer, a lady postmistress by the name of Mary

Ann Hughes, who lived near Pen Dam at a house called Tan y Bryn. She took her duties very seriously. Later a man called Chris Sandford who lived at Penrhiw would do her work.

Dick the Post would make his way over Penrhiw, following the route we went to school, and on to the post-office at Penbontrhydybeddau or Penbont for short. There he would meet another part-timer, Dick Evans, whose wife kept the post-office, and their son Wynford lived with them too. Dick Evans would now go to Cwmerfyn and Bank y Daren and all farms in between. Dick the Post would then do the last lap from Penbont to Cwmsymlog village, about a mile and a half further on. At the end of the long journey was a hut provided by the GPO where the postman could rest before starting the return journey. There was a small fireplace where the postman could light a fire in order to boil a kettle for a well-earned cuppa.

He would then start the long journey back to Bow Street, collecting all the mail from post boxes along the way. His timing was immaculate and many people would rely entirely on Dick the post's footsteps for their time checks. I can recall being let off school early one day, perhaps because of a snowstorm threatening, and trying to keep up with Dick up Banc Tyngelli – but it was almost an impossible task. Many a time I saw icicles hanging off his walrus moustache – past his mouth at times. He worked six days a week for forty years and the only help he got was at Christmas time when his son David, who had a saddler's shop in Aberystwyth and also ran a motorcycle and sidecar, would run a consignment of Christmas parcels ahead of him, dropping them off at various junctions en route to await his arrival to deliver them locally (the passage in our house in Salem was one of these depositories). When Dick retired it was obvious that no replacement of his calibre would ever be found. The GPO therefore experimented with a man on a bicycle doing the same journey, but this was soon found to be, if anything, worse than the daily hike, since in those days a post-office bike was a very heavy affair, with a basket in front to carry a heavy mail bag and waterproofs. Imagine, therefore, trying to hump this contraption round from Salem to Penbont – and he could never take it down Banc Tyngelli.

The GPO thought again, and came up with the idea of a motorcycle combination. Two BSA 250s were bought for the job (one of them for reserve) and a man from Bow Street, Bill Hughes, had the job for a few years. It was a very smart turnout, with a bright red sidecar and a rider with a peaked cap (no crash helmet in those days). This method of distributing the post continued until probably just before the beginning of the war, when it was then replaced by the popular Morris 8 red vans. Bill Hughes and his wife retired next door to us in Penrhyn-coch in about 1948.

* * *

John Davy's garden had two chicken coops enclosed in a wire-netting run. My friend Ifor and I were entrusted with one coop each to look after. At first we didn't have chickens but pet rabbits. Mine was a slate blue chinchilla, and from these we bred litters of small rabbits which we passed on to friends. We also took some of them to various horticultural shows around the area, with varied results. I can't recall making much profit from these ventures, though we bought many a three pennies worth of bran etc. for them, to supplement their diet of dandelion leaves. Eventually, however, we moved on to keeping chickens. I had various breeds including some bantams. We had made a hole in the hedge from the chicken run into the adjoining field, allowing the chickens to graze there and return to roost at night in the coops.

Ifor had some Rhode Island Reds, among them was a huge cockerel, and I remember that my bantam cock was certainly the boss of all of them when out in the field. He would jump on the red cockerel's back and ride him like a jockey much to our amusement.

* * *

Among our regular annual events to look forward to was New Year's Day or Dydd Calan. It was the custom in most parts of rural Wales for children to go round from dawn until midday to wish the occupants a Happy New Year. In return, each child would receive some *calennig*, a penny usually or some sweets. Some people would take this very seriously and beforehand would have arranged to have a stock of brand new pennies laid out in readiness for the day. Parents would make a drawstring or tape cotton bag, which would be hung around our necks to carry the *calennig* and, on our return around midday, there would be much counting and comparing of proceeds to see who had most and then deciding how to spend it. It was also customary to go around in a group of about five or six for this activity – not too many and not too few in number – as we had learnt from past experience that it was most important to derive the maximum benefit. The various groups would each take a different course around the villages and, at some point, would meet up with another group on the same mission.

The song that we would sing at each house however would be the same – one that had been handed down to us over the generations. This would say that another New Year had arrived and that we wished it to be a happy one for the occupants, and invited them to come to the door cheerfully whilst reminding them that before we would see another New Year many would be in their graves. This was called singing for *calennig*, and it might have varied slightly from area to area, but generally it remained the same. By now the old custom has *almost* died out.

I can remember calling at a house in Penrhyn-coch where an English family lived. Outside the garden gate on that morning an emergency 'committee' was formed to decide what we would sing, as we knew that they would not understand our usual rendering. So, it was decided that we would give them the hymn 'Our God our help in ages past'. I cannot recall what reception we had, apart from a lot of amusement when we arrived home to tell our parents what we had done.

Another of my regular outings was to visit my grandmother in her house called Cwarel near Capel Madog – it was quite a walk crossing two valleys diagonally. She lived there with my aunt, Sara or Auntie Sal, as we would call her. Auntie Sal did some sewing and quilting to supplement her income. Now and again she would get an order for a quilt to be made for someone's wedding present. During the weeks that it would take her to make the quilt, it would be difficult to cross the living room and often one had to get on hands and knees to cross the room underneath the quilt in construction. The quilt was held by 3" x 2" poles, some 8 foot long with stretchers to hold them about 2 foot apart; the remainder of the quilt was rolled around the poles in turn and quilted in between. It was a very long and tedious job but obviously paid for anyone with lots of patience and interest in the art. These quilts were very popular wedding presents in those days. And, during the 1980s there were adverts in the press offering good prices for second-hand quilts in good condition.

But my grandmother did nothing to contribute to the quilting process, other than sit on her hard, high-back chair by the fire feeling very sorry for herself. She lived until the 1950s, moving down to a little cottage in Capel Dewi, a much more convenient place which made it easier to visit as it was now on the bus route.

As mentioned earlier, we were the only private house in Salem during my childhood which reared a pig. In early spring, my mother would go to Aberystwyth to buy a piglet. It was customary in those days for farmers on a Monday, the market day, to take their pig litters to town. Farmers would park their carts with a net covering the little pigs around the old market hall. There would usually be much haggling over price, and my mother would eventually return home with a very noisy piglet in a sack, placed behind the rear seat on the bus. It would then be let loose in our pigsty; bracken from the nearby banks was suitable bedding for it.

Neighbours would pass judgement on the latest arrival and soon there would be offerings of food, such as leftovers to potato peelings and, in no time at all, the little pig would be thriving. It was my duty to clean out his bedding and the dump or *domen* alongside the sty would gradually grow in readiness for gardening the following spring, and the starting of the whole process all over again.

However, about November, when my mother would say the weather would have cooled down enough, an old friend of hers, Dick Edwards, who still lived in Cefnllwyd near my grandmother's house, would be summoned to kill the pig and prepare it for salting and storage. He wouldn't arrive until all of us had left for school. The pig was, by now, a kind of a pet. By the time we'd arrive back home in the afternoon, the pig would be hanging by his hind legs, scalded and shaved in the back kitchen. The process of cutting the carcass up into manageable portions to be salted wouldn't start until towards dusk, as the carcass needed to cool down. My first job after tea was to go to the shop and borrow the large hanging weighing scales to weigh the carcass. Dick Edwards, with the help of one or two neighbours, would declare the weight like a prize fighter being weighed in – except that the weight was always given in scores. A few days earlier I would've had the job of wheeling a very large block of salt from the shop to the house. The cutting up would now begin and we would all work flat out. The small pieces of the pig, such as the backbone together with the liver and even the head and the trotters, would be distributed among the local neighbours in return for the scraps that they'd given to feed the pig when it was alive. For days, while walking from one end of the village to the other, one would smell roasting pork coming from every house, and one would begin to realize that Christmas was not very far away. Meat such as hams and sides of bacon would be salted and left in a wooden tub under the back kitchen table for a couple of weeks. Then they would be lifted out and hung up on hooks protruding from the ceiling which almost every house had in its kitchens in those days. From there on the meat was sliced as it was required, and very good it was too.

As already mentioned, when I was about 12 or 13 years of age, my ten-year-old sister Megan met a very unfortunate accident. She was bitten by a dog just below the kneecap. It didn't seem to heal, despite the usual home medication, and became badly swollen. My mother, as with the usual habit of the time, didn't show it to a doctor probably fearing the hefty bill that would inevitably follow. However, she showed it to the passing district nurse, who in innocence rather than ignorance, and wanting to be helpful, gave the affected knee a thorough massage.

Following an appointment with an eminent orthopaedic surgeon, my mother was told that that was the worse thing that could have been done to the knee. He illustrated his point by saying that if there was a rotten spot in an orange one would not rub or massage the orange as the inevitable would happen. However, the damage was done, and Megan was admitted to a north Wales hospital specialising in TB bones at Llangwyfan near Denbigh, where the knee joint would be operated on and hopefully cured. Megan had to lie in bed on her back for 18 months. It was very difficult for any of us to visit her at this time, as the hospital was some 80 miles away and there was no convenient public transport. The only way was to hire a car or get a taxi for the day, though we couldn't do this very often because of the cost. She was eventually cured but had lost the joint from her knee, but managed well afterwards.

My elder sister, Hannah Mary, was at Ardwyn County School in Aberystwyth, lodging with a distant aunt and coming home every weekend. However, she developed the dreaded TB which was very prevalent in those days, and she also had to be admitted to Llangwyfan Sanatorium where she remained for some time, before returning to us in Salem not having made the recovery that was hoped for. She lived in very poor health until 1937 when she died at the age of 20, and was buried in Salem Chapel cemetery.

There were many similar tragic cases during those years, probably due to living conditions at the time and the lack of an early diagnosis of this dreaded disease.

5

Employment

MY FATHER EVENTUALLY gave up coal mining in south Wales and returned home. He suffered from a bad chest and hoped to find a local job, but it was now the depths of the depression in the early 1930s and things were very bad.

The County Council tried to do something to help local workers, and decided on a road widening scheme: the road running from Bow Street to Lovesgrove flats through Capel Dewi. This improvement scheme was done before the advent of modern machinery such as earth moving and bulldozing machines, so it very labour intensive. Anyone with any kind of lorry, or what could be turned into a small lorry, had the job of hauling stones from the old mine tips at Cwmsymlog to the site. But, had there been an MOT in those days, inspectors would have had a field day examining all those so-called lorries which were traversing daily. Men, including my father, had the job of digging the new road and laying all the stone foundation by hand. It was a poorly paid job – but it was a job, and better than being on the dole and it did ensure that one's card was stamped for future dole claims.

I was now fourteen and could leave school. Like most boys of my age, I was anxious to do so and to get a job and contribute towards my keep. Mr Dan Jones, my old schoolmaster, had made every effort to persuade me to sit the entrance exam for the secondary school, but my mind was made up – my mother had already sacrificed enough.

I was very reluctant to go along with the crowd and work for local farmers for some pittance or other. Many from my age group were forced to, but I persuaded my father to come with me to see if I could find work in Aberystwyth. I wanted work which involved something electrical or mechanical, as they were my main interests. It was a fruitless search until we reached W H Jones & Son, Great Darkgate Street, an ironmongers and china store which had recently opened another department, a wireless section, as it was known in those days. They offered to take me on and teach me wireless operations under the guidance of H G Snell, who had studied to be a sea-going radio operator, but had failed the eye test and had to fall back on this job. Wireless operations in those days were just past infancy and, despite the fact that there were plenty of factory-made sets available everywhere, a large slice of the market was still do-it-yourself enthusiasts. These were very simple, as various parts were available from over the counter at most high street shops. They were made up to some particular design by following diagrams and instructions in technical periodicals of the time. As time went on more and more ready-made sets became available and were, therefore, cheaper. This was a job that pleased me a great deal and I was offered half a crown (12½p) per week for my services, which was soon doubled to five shillings or 25p today. Ifor, my childhood friend also found a job in the hardware department of the same shop.

Our main problem now was finding somewhere to stay: the shop in those days remained open until 7 p.m. or 7.30 p.m. on weekday evenings and until 8 p.m. to 8.30 p.m. on Saturdays, and we had started each morning at 8.30 a.m. Luck would have it that Beattie, my sister, was now in domestic service with an elderly couple named Dei and Sal Morgan at Ger y Llan, Grey's Inn Road. It was a big house which used to be a pub called the Three Horse Shoes.

Ifor and I abandoned any thoughts of cycling in to work every day, and we were offered an attic bedroom to share in Ger y Llan for 5 shillings a week each, providing our own food of course, which Beattie would cook for us. Therefore the five shillings I would earn at W H Jones went to pay for lodgings, and my parents still had to pay for my food! During the season this was supplemented by garden and farm produce when we could find the means to transport it from Salem. Any other luxury, such as a night at the cinema, would have to come from various tips we would receive doing little jobs or errands at work.

We bicycled home every Saturday night after the shop closed no matter what the weather was, in the pitch darkness and back again for 8.30 on Monday morning. We also went home on Wednesday half-day too.

One of my duties during those years was charging batteries in the cellar of the shop. There was no electricity supply outside the town boundary in those days, and all wireless sets therefore were battery operated. This consisted of a single-cell accumulator of two volts of varying size and a dry high-tension battery. The accumulator would give a couple of weeks' worth of normal use, then it would have to be taken into the shop to be recharged, which would take a couple of days. So everybody had two batteries for the switch over. The dry battery would normally last about three months depending on the amount of use it had. We would have a bench in the cellar at W H Jones with over a hundred batteries bubbling and gassing away, connected to a large battery charger, with a stream of customers coming and going with their batteries to be recharged and collected. The price for charging a battery was sixpence. The service was quite profitable to the shopkeeper as it brought a constant stream of customers through his shop every day. And one had to be very careful in handling these accumulators as they contained sulphuric acid which ruined clothes if it splashed on them.

One had to marvel at the service this shop gave in those days. I recall being given the task of delivering these accumulators on an old carrier bike to almost every part of the town and sometimes beyond, and the charge would still be only sixpence! Ifor, in the shop next door, would also have to deliver say a gallon of paraffin anywhere in town by the same means, with the price of a gallon of paraffin being around one shilling.

Wireless reception in those days was, compared to today, very poor, particularly in Cardiganshire and west Wales as there wasn't a radio station in Wales. We had to depend on a station in Clevedon, across the Bristol Channel, even for the few Welsh programmes and, after dark, the interference and fading would be considerable. We often received our Medium Wave or Home Service from Belfast, as the weakness of the signal over water was far less than over the mountains of Wales. To try to overcome this, the best type of aerial was erected as high as possible and clear of any obstacles. Therefore, everybody would have an aerial wire strung between two chimney stacks or from a high pole at the end of the garden and leading to the living room.

Part of my job was to erect some of those aerials. How I managed not to break my neck during those years is a mystery. Still, I suppose familiarity and practice won the day, and I climbed some of the highest houses and buildings in town to put those aerials in place. All I know is that I couldn't do it now! I had a couple of extension ladders and a roof ladder and the use of a hand cart to push them around the town to wherever the job was. There were no convenient vans or pick-ups for transport then.

I recall my own attempt at making one of these home-made wireless sets from components scrounged from work; then, the erection of an aerial and its installation in Salem. The loudspeaker was a Swan Neck Horn variety, again found from somewhere, and I can only guess that I managed to save enough to purchase the necessary batteries to operate the thing much to everyone's amazement!

Radios became more and more popular and before very long we'd managed to purchase a better second-hand one that served us well for years. The first good set in Salem was purchased by John Davy – some people would say that it was to compensate for the loss of both Ifor and me from under his feet all day! However, as with all his other purchases, this radio had to be the very best available. He came to W H Jones, and purchased a Pye portable. Portable was not really the correct description for it, apart from the fact that it did not need an aerial. John Davy's set was quite large, something resembling the size of the average TV set today and battery operated. It cost fourteen guineas.

There were quite a variety of programmes on the radio which we would all follow intently. I remember listening to the Hitler's Nuremberg rallies, though I didn't understand them, which gave us an indication of what was to come. There was a weekly Welsh religious service broadcast each Sunday morning around 11 a.m. from a different church or chapel. These were eagerly anticipated and often discussed afterwards.

Those were the 1930s and there was every indication that a war was on the horizon – so and so had joined up, and so it went on and on. The only other news to break the monotony of the forthcoming gloom was the abdication of King Edward to marry an American divorcee.

6

The Coming of War

LIKE EVERY OTHER 19-year-old in the summer of 1939, I had to register for National Service. Firstly we had to attend the Drill Hall in Aberystwyth for a medical. I then waited for my first call-up papers to come, and reported in September 1939 to Kinmel Bay camp in north Wales to join a searchlight unit. However, when the war was declared on the 3 September these instructions were cancelled and I was to await further orders.

During June of that year there'd been great excitement in Aberystwyth when two Navy battleships and a destroyer came to visit. One was called *Renown* and the other *The Prince of Wales*. As usual during those summer visits the town and surrounding areas were heaving with sailors on shore leave. Dances and entertainment were organized to welcome them. However, one night during this particular visit, a signal was flashed that all the sailors had to be back on board by 6 a.m. By the time the town had woken up the following morning, all the ships were gone and the bay was empty again. This was the first indication that war mobilization had begun.

From then on there were frantic preparations. Surface bomb shelters were built everywhere, emergency water tanks erected, the occasional blackout at night, air raid sirens tested, until the end of August when the biggest trial of all was scheduled – the arrival of the evacuees. Aberystwyth received evacuees from Liverpool. They came in their thousands, mostly small children, school by school with their teachers and were billeted in the town and countryside all around. There were some humorous *and* some tragic scenes those days. Most of these children had never seen the countryside before, nor had they been away from the back streets of Liverpool. As you can well imagine, having left their parents behind and then in new surroundings, there was much fretting and wetting of beds, and it was a familiar sight to see the bin lorry or cart going to the tip with a pile of ruined mattresses.

Some evacuees took to their new surroundings very well and a lot of them spoke Welsh eventually. I can still remember them arriving, each carrying their little bag of travel rations and inevitable newly-issued gas mask in its cardboard box slung over their shoulders. Coupled with all this upheaval was the fact that rationing was soon to begin and everyone had to have their own ration book. And it wasn't just food that was rationed, but clothes, shoes, soft furnishings, bed linen and petrol too.

Although I was to be out of it very soon, I can only look back in admiration at the organization of it all – long before computers and modern radio telephone communications came into being.

Not only did Liverpool evacuees arrive in Aberystwyth but, like every other safe haven, we also saw rich people from large cities taking over each vacant property. All nationalities were to be seen shopping around the town. Large numbers never went back after the war and some of their families and descendants still live in the area to this day.

However I just had to wait to see what would happen to me. Ifor, who was a few months older than me, had already been called up. On 15 December 1939, my turn came when I had to report to the Royal Artillery Anti-Aircraft (RAAA) camp at Oswestry to start quite a different chapter in my life.

7

The War Years – Basic Training

I ENLISTED DAY at Park Hall, 110 Anti-Aircraft (AA) Training Region, Oswestry. It was with some trepidation that I entered this newly-built camp, a mile and a half outside Oswestry. It was built of wood in a spider-block style: this meant that the ablution block (with showers/washbasins/toilets) was in the middle, with six barrack rooms around that. They had wooden walls and floors and central heating, with twenty single beds per room and one enclosed non-commissioned officer's (NCO) room at the end. All in all, it was very comfortable. We guessed that much of our time for the next few weeks would be spent outside, however. On arrival we had another medical inspection and were issued an Army number which would follow me until I was eventually released. Mine is etched into my memory: 1533601. But, as was usual in the services, I was known by the last three digits which followed my name: Davies 601.

The days that followed were busy with inoculations, the issue of my first uniform, including a service gas mask (in exchange for the civilian one which had been distributed to everybody during the previous summer). Also, we were given an Army pay book which we were to carry around at all times and show on demand. We all handed a large sheet of brown paper and string to pack our civilian clothes away, which would be forwarded to our homes in due course. We were now soldiers of the King and looked alike, despite the poor fit of some of the uniforms issued to us.

We lived in a modern barracks and the dining hall was equally modern. We ate from china plates and mugs and when the bugle sounded 'cookhouse' or dinner time, the only thing we had to bring was what the Army called 'eating irons', that is a knife, fork and spoon – everybody looked after them very carefully. The days of enamel mugs and mess tins were yet to come.

The days leading up to Christmas 1939 were very cold with snow showers. However, we were kept busy and warm by marching up and down, doing PT, and route marching, map reading and cross country running, during which we saw quite a bit of the countryside around Oswestry, Chirk and Gobowen.

On Sunday afternoons we would wander up to the well-known Gobowen Sanatorium to chat to some of the patients whose beds had been wheeled out to the verandas for a bit of fresh air. They would consider it a treat to talk to the young soldiers.

We also had a cinema at the camp to entertain us and another was located in town. There was also the NAAFI (Navy, Army and Air Force Institutes) with its piano. A new intake of recruits came to the camp each month. Initial training took about three months and the history of military training down through the ages was taught to us too. We would note the awkwardness of the latest intake being put through their drill, not realizing that we looked probably equally uncomfortable only a few weeks earlier.

One Sunday evening I recall feeling very groggy with a sore throat and raging temperature. A newly-promoted Lance Bombardier told me to put my greatcoat on and marched me to a medical camp, about half a mile away. On arrival, the poor bloke, in all his innocence was given a severe dressing down by the Medical Orderly Sergeant (MOS) and shown the empty ambulances standing in a row outside and asked what the **** did he think they were for? I must say I felt rather sorry for him, but after a few days of Army medication I was back to training – more marching and rifle drill, PT, and instruction in small arms. This meant classroom lectures about the Lee Enfield rifle, the Bren gun, Bigs antitank rifle, Lewis machine gun, Tommy gun and the hand grenade. In those early days of the war the main emphasis was on defence against an air attack and the main weapon for this was the 3.7 anti-aircraft gun, so training was mainly directed at this gun. Even before the outbreak of war, there was an important firing practice installation for this on the coast at Tonfannau near Tywyn; that firing often rattled the windows in Salem during heavy barrages.

After my enlistment I tried to transfer to some job which would benefit my civilian work later – anything to do with radio or electrical. But, it was to no avail, until eighteen months later when I had a breakthrough.

Laying a gun on a fast-moving target such as an aeroplane required a number of calculations to be made. Remember, this was the age before the discovery of computers. The only aid to gun layers was a predictor, which was a very complicated instrument combining visual and mechanical calculation of the speed etc. of the target, worked out in conjunction with another complicated instrument called the height-finder. The predictor was an instrument about the size of two modern TV sets, while the height-finder was cylindrical and about 6 to 8 feet long; both were free standing quite and worked by a small petrol generator.

Operators for these complicated instruments were chosen during early training, by selecting those who'd had a good secondary school record. Therefore, Davies 601 was out of it again, as I was a mere product of Trefeurig School. I was left to fill other jobs such as passing the ammunition and moving the machine guns. At the end of three months' training we were indeed moved on as a battery to the already mentioned Tonfannau range to practice firing at actual targets. As I hadn't had training in manning the 3.7 gun, I was left to do odd jobs in our billets, which were a number of the large houses on the promenade at Tywyn. However, being so close to home meant that my girlfriend Lena could come up to see me during her half-day; she was working in an Aberystwyth shop, before doing some National Service herself later.

Later, news came that we would be posted to an active service unit. It was now April 1940. I was posted to 115 Light AA Battery at Derby. This was a sort of Territorial Army unit from around Derby and its commanding officer was Viscount Scarsdale from Kedleston Hall nearby. He was a fine gentleman who stuttered badly, especially when addressing his troops. He was a bit of a boxing fanatic too as were a number of his senior NCOs who had broken noses and cauliflower ears etc.! Viscount Scarsdale kept his favourite Golden Labrador by his side most of the time too.

We were a Light AA Battery but, as was often the case in those early war years, there were not enough guns to go round. So, the Northern Command had to find us something to do with our time. We were moved around to several locations during the early summer of 1940, using Lewis guns from the First World War on the pretext that we were guarding some vulnerable spot such as a railway junction. Later we were deployed on the roof of the Birtley Ordinance Factory. It was there that I heard of the evacuation at Dunkirk and of Winston Churchill becoming Prime Minister. We moved on to other sites too, from Seaham Harbour to Gateshead near Newcastle-upon-Tyne, but still with no proper guns. If only Hitler had known!

We were eventually ordered to go to Redcar in North Yorkshire to guard the steelworks of Dorman Longs which was busy making Bailey bridges. The Army considered them vital for the war effort and rightly so. Up until then there hadn't been any local air raids, but on the outer ring of Redcar a series of 4.5 guns or heavy AA were deployed; on the next a ring, 3.7; and close to the factory, a ring of 3" old naval guns, bedded into the surrounding slag heaps. The gun emplacements made of sandbags were a square shape, and we had to sleep in tents next to the guns, with a sergeant in charge of each gun site. But as we were short of men to man all the guns in that particular location, the Army allowed some Royal Marine reinforcements and as the guns were ex-naval, it was assumed that they would be familiar with them. Far from it – and we *all* had to learn as we went along. The guns, although old, were excellent. We practised and practised and the best reward and amusement was to scan the sand dunes along Redcar's golf course with the gun's telescopic sight – much to the annoyance of various courting couples!

Looking out to sea from our high point on top of the slag heap, we could see the colliery ships taking coal down the River Tees and out into the bay. We watched them through our guns' telescopic sights and also sat in the spotter's chair, which was popular on all AA sites. The spotter's chair was a swivel deckchair made of varnished wood slats where one could recline and look through binoculars for planes in the sky. There was one spotters chair to every gun site. One day we were looking at a coal ship sailing down the coast when there was a huge bang and a flash and the ship was no more; it had probably struck a mine dropped from the air by a German plane the night before. For the next few days hundreds of tons of coal covered the beach alongside the golf club, and scores of people came with carts and wheelbarrows from all around to carry the coal away.

A few nights later the siren went off again and we stood to. The searchlights were mounted and suddenly they caught a Dornier aeroplane not very far offshore, dropping more mines to catch shipping. All guns were trained on the plane; we were instructed not to fire unless fired upon for two reasons: one, we were not properly trained and two, ammunition was very scarce. The gun next to us was located in the yard of the steelworks, and the Marine loading the gun pulled out the shell and clipped the fuse a few points and then reloaded. With such a perfect target he could stand it no longer, and yanked the cord which operated the firing lever. The cord was very old and broke in his hand. Not to be outdone, he put his hand up along the breach and pulled the lever by hand. The gun fired and the shell took the top of a telephone post with it and went on to explode very close to the tail plane of the Dornier, which immediately plummeted down to the sea. We were all too shocked to cheer...

The following morning we were on parade in the steelworks' yard and every brass hat from the General down was there to interview the Marine. There was question after question: What height was the plane? What fuse did he use? On and on. I can remember them all smiling at each other. I still do not know to this day whether that was the first enemy aircraft to be brought down by AA during the war.

Later, the brass hats at HQ decided to arrange for a spitfire to buzz our gun site, flying low and at a very high speed. We watched it coming from a brilliant blue sky towards the gun and then back up again. The updraught it caused took both of our India Pattern tents and fly sheets with it, scattering our kit all over the place. It must have been good fun for the pilot.

News of an impending move soon spread and we moved again to Derby, the unit's home base. We took up station at a park on the outskirts of the city, Normanton's recreational ground. It was pretty much the same set up, the big boys in the outer circle next to the 3.7 gun and my detachment manning a Bofors gun in the middle of the park alongside a detachment of RAF men manning a balloon barrage site. The reason for all this was that the Rolls Royce Company were making the famous Merlin engine for aeroplanes in Derby at that time – we could hear these engines being tested day and night. We slept in tents under the trees in the park and ate food sent to us from the park warden's hut. The Rolls Royce factory was considered to be so important that every moonlit night the smoke generators were opened all over the city which covered the place in an oily, smelling fog and you could hardly see your hand in front of you in the blackout.

Nevertheless, it was a very pleasant site for us to stay at and at weekends dozens of local people would stand around the perimeter fence watching Sergeant Webster, minus his teeth, giving us gun drill. The spectators would also bring various comforts such as cakes and magazines and invited one or two of us out to supper.

I'm writing these memoirs as an octogenarian. It's hard sometimes to put it all in the correct order and I have regretted many a time that I did not keep a diary. Such a habit was not encouraged then, in fact frowned on, as were photographs, lest they fall into enemy hands later. Throughout my service years, letters from home were the best sort of entertainment. My mother was always very keen for me to meet up with anyone from the Aberystwyth area when I was away from home. A letter would come from her, for instance, with news that she'd been to town the day before and had met Mary Jane, who had told her that her daughter's husband's brother was stationed not very far from me and urging me to go and see him as soon as possible. Early on I followed these recommendations even when I realised that I wouldn't have known the person anyway, and that he was based quite a distance from me. But after a while I grew weary and my mother gave up in the end, though it kept her busy for many months trying to make the connections. I heard from Lena constantly of course and my sisters and aunties kept in touch fairly regularly.

My next move was to Lincolnshire in the autumn of 1940 to help guard Hemswell No. 1 bomber station, from where Hampden bombers flew almost every night to Germany. The Local Defence Volunteers (LDV) which later became the Home Guard, protected the aerodrome and we had a variety of small machine guns to help discourage air attacks. We were billeted in the old barracks of the airfield, in old wooden Nissen huts. This part was infested with rats, so we did not sleep very well at first. The only job I had while stationed at Hemswell was as a telephone operator: all the gun sites around the aerodrome were connected by a ten-line switchboard situated in a sandbagged dug-out on the roof of the station's operations room. It was 24 hours on and then 24 hours off. On my days off, I would hitchhike to Lincoln, some 10 to 15 miles due south, or to Gainsborough, slightly nearer and due west.

Being so near to the operations room meant I could see all the comings and goings – the briefings before setting off for Germany and debriefings on their return in the early morning. On some nights, alone in my position, the operations commander would ring me and ask me to step out onto the flat roof at about five or six in the morning to listen out for the sound of a plane in trouble. I would go down for breakfast later and listen to the BBC news on the radio: "We bombed Hamburg last night, and many of our planes are missing." One felt very close to the events on those days. The crew would fuel and load up their bombs during the afternoon, but might not set off until after 10 p.m. In the meantime they would park their bombers in the dispersal areas on the perimeter of the airfield near to our AA guns.

In order to keep their aeroplane engines warm, there was a stove under the canvas canopy to keep them so. One night, a gust of wind blew the canopy off and it caught fire from the oil stove. The plane was fully fuelled and had bombs on board and quickly went up in flames. The gunners helped put the fire out. But, not before one of the lads shouted "keep it going for a bit"! He ran as fast as he could to his tent to fetch his overcoat. When he had joined the Army, he had been issued with what we used to call a 'maternity' coat, a single-breasted version of a First World War vintage, and he had been trying to get it changed ever since. So the fire was eventually extinguished with the aid of this Army coat! It was amusing to see the RAF notice board highly commending the brave gunner for saving the bomber and its load; it was valued at many thousands of pounds, and all for the cost of one Army coat. One of the aircrew, Sergeant Hannah, won the VC while we were there for heroic action bombing Germany. There were several airfields dotted around Lincolnshire in those days, even before the Americans entered the war.

Late that autumn, around November 1940, our superiors thought it was time for our Battery to prove themselves on the Bofors 40mm gun at a firing range in north-west England. This was Cark-in-Cartmel near Grange-over-Sands, slightly south of Barrow-in-Furness. By the time we got there winter was descending. Snow and strong winds were problematic every night and the Nissen cookhouse nearly uprooted more than once.

We were practising at a target towed behind a plane. When it was my turn to be the layer on the predictor we had our first direct hit. The gun was connected to the predictor by a heavy cable and would follow the instructions of the predictor at all times. Another member of the team was the loader, who would drop a clip of four shells into the breach whilst standing on the loading platform with his foot on the firing pedal, while other members passed him more ammunition. Each 40mm shell was a tracer shell, which meant that its base would glow in dark conditions after leaving the barrel. It was quite a sight to see a string of these shells streaking across the sky towards its cloth target. As was customary after a good hit, the towing plane would turn around and drop the target close to the gunners as a souvenir: I had a piece of the red cloth target to take home with me.

When I next returned home on leave, Meurig Magor, my nephew, who was then at Ardwyn School, had been hit by a car. He'd been walking at night in the blackout on a road near his home in Llandre and was now seriously ill in hospital. When I went to see him, his first request was whether he could have the piece of the cloth target that I had helped to shoot down. He kept it for years and it was given back to me not long before Sal's (his mother and my sister) death and I have still got it.

Despite the atrocious weather in Cark, a group of us managed to walk across the sands one night to the cinema at

Grange. This was a small town on the coast though, in the dark, I did not see much of it. I remember that we received a great welcome. The manager of this little cinema came to the door to welcome us, and did not charge any of us for entry.

Two weeks at the firing range soon passed. We heard that things were looking bad in the Western Desert, with our forces were falling back under General Wavell. However our commanding officer, the Viscount, received an urgent order one day to put us all on a train for Southend-on-Sea where further instructions would be waiting for us. There was no transport to take us to the station, so we had to march with Full Service Marching Order with the Major and his Golden Labrador leading the way in the pouring rain. All we needed now was a military band to play the '1812 Overture' and it would have been the re-enactment of Napoléon's retreat from Moscow. We travelled all night to London before stopping at a siding on the outskirts when an air raid was expected. As we weren't provided with refreshments we were famished by the time we arrived at Southend about 8 a.m. Our CO took the lead again and he marched us up the main street of Southend until we came to a cinema. There we saw a woman cleaning the brass work in the entrance. The CO asked her to get the manager, who allowed us to sit down inside the cinema. He later went to rouse the organist who played a melody to entertain us while the Major went to get further instructions from the War Office.

When he returned he took us all across the road to a restaurant to have breakfast. Then we marched two or three miles to Westcliff-on-Sea and occupied some empty houses along the front. We settled in and marched back to Southend for lunch, or tiffin as it was called in the Army. Then back to Westcliff and to and fro like this for several days until it seemed that all that we were doing was eating and marching all day. The Army eventually commandeered a small garage and set up a cookhouse. An orderly room was set up in another house nearby and we were now all set for further training.

During our stay in Southend an air raid and landmine completely demolished the cinema in which we'd sheltered only a few weeks earlier. We tried to make ourselves as comfortable as possible in the empty houses, and slept on the floors. The Army allowed us coal to keep a fire going in each house. We were marched once a week to Southend to have a bath in the public baths, close to the pier. One day, as we marched back to our billets, we witnessed a first-class dogfight in the sky. An ME 109 was hovering around and a spitfire came out of nowhere: one burst and down came the 109, just missing the end of the pier. We certainly had a grandstand view that day.

In Southend there was an epidemic of sore throats. The Army command were very concerned and ordered everybody to gargle Condis Fluid every morning. The commanding officer lined up all his men in a little park nearby. There'd been a dusting of snow the night before and it had frozen hard. We'd brought our mugs and the orderlies carried the Condis Fluid in two buckets. They poured the liquid into each mug and we all gargled together. As we marched out of the park to get our breakfast, there were two long lines of mauve pools where we had stood and spat out the gargle in the snow. Little incidents like that stick in one's mind for ever, I suppose.

Soon there was talk of us going overseas and this was confirmed when we were all issued with tropical kit, such as Khaki Drill (KD) slacks and a Topi (large sunhat) etc. We were given embarkation leave of seven days. I went home and shall never forget the return journey to Southend through London. The Blitz meant stops and starts to the journey, detours, and no refreshments. My mother had baked me a fruitcake to go back with, but I'd eaten it all by the time I arrived back at the billet.

Not long after my return I was told that I'd been posted and was to hand in my tropical kit and go to Woolwich, to the old Royal Artillery barracks which was a transit camp in those days. I was there for about two weeks and, to pass the time, they would march us around the common with the famous

Royal Artillery band leading us. During the evening we had to do picket duty, taking walks around Woolwich Common and keeping an eye open for parachutists. There were concrete pillboxes dotted around the common. They held petrol bombs, known in those days as Molotov Cocktails, after the famous Russian minister. In the event of an invasion, we were to throw these at the enemy. We had no other arms; we were in a right state at the time.

Very soon, however, my next posting came through which proved that consistently in applying for a transfer was bearing fruit at last. I was to be sent on a four-month wireless mechanic course at a Northampton technical college. When I arrived there I met many like myself who had been in the trade pre-war, but there were also quite a few who had no experience of wireless operations. We'd been gathered from all over the country and regiments, some 30 to 40 in all.

We were housed in private billets; I lived with the Adams family in a street not very far from the college. Mrs Adams was an excellent cook and fed us very well bearing in mind that rationing was going on. Mr Adams was close to retiring age, having worked all his life as a shoemaker in one of the famous shoe factories in town. Their son John still attended school. The college was primarily for teaching shoemaking skills in peace time, but also taught the care and maintenance of electric motors. There was an excellent workshop/laboratory for this purpose at the college. We had two instructors during the course – one had been at the Marian Marine College in Colwyn Bay with Hedley Snell, the man who had taught me everything I knew about radio. A strange coincidence! The other was an ex-Naval telegraphist.

We didn't have to take part in any parades, kit inspections, guard duty etc. while on the course. The only duty we were made to perform, especially at weekends and bank holidays, was fire watching. It meant patrolling the premises and rooftops to make sure that no incendiary bombs were dropped by passing enemy planes unnoticed. I remember

John David Rees collecting manure for his rhubarb. John Davy, as he was affectionately known, was a surrogate father to Elfed during the times when his father was working in the south Wales coalmines.

Salem Chapel, first built in 1824 and extended several times since. This photograph was taken in 1924.

Salem Band of Hope in 1922. Elfed is fifth on the right in the front row. Boys were certainly outnumbered by girls in the community.

Farm residents and children from Salem in 1932. Elfed is third on the right in the second row. Everyone is wearing Sunday best for this photograph.

Elfed and his mother shopping on Great Darkgate Street, Aberystwyth around 1932. His friend Ifor James accompanies them – plenty of people and no cars to be seen.

Elfed's parents, Marged Ann and John Davies. They were married in 1906 and had seven children.

Elfed and Ifor James in Salem in 1932. Vehicles in the hamlet were a novelty then and attracted much attention.

The Terrace, Salem in 1950. Tŷ Marged Ann is the first on the right. The garden is no longer there.

MILITARY TRAINING ACT, 1939

GRADE CARD

Registration No. _ACK 294_

Mr. _William Elfed Davies_

whose address on his registration card is

23 Grays Inn Rd.   Aberystwyth.

was medically examined at DRILL HALL,

ABERYSTWYTH.

on _1 2 JUL 1939_

and placed in

GRADE* _I.   ONE._

E.D. Until*

ABERYSTWYTH
MEDICAL BOARD
(Medical Board stamp)

Chairman of Board _David Elias_

Man's Signature _Wm. Elfed Davies._

*The roman numeral denoting the man's Grade (with number also spelt out) will be entered in RED ink by the Chairman himself, e.g., Grade I (one), Grade II (two) (a) (Vision). If the examination is deferred the Chairman will enter a date after the words " E.D. Until ", and cross out " Grade " ; alternatively, the words " E.D. Until........ " will be struck out.

M.R. 55   [P.T.O.

During the summer of 1939 all 19-year-old boys had to report to the Drill Hall in Aberystwyth. A card to prove that Elfed passed his medical for the armed forces.

MILITARY TRAINING ACT, 1939

Ministry of Labour,

Employment Exchange,

ABERYSTWYTH

Date_____ 16 AUG '39

Mr. *W. E. Davies,*
23, Grays Inn Road,
ABERYSTWYTH

Registration No. *ACK 294 V*

Dear Sir,

In accordance with the Military Training Act, 1939, you will be required to present yourself for military training on *Tuesday* *10th* day *October* 19*39*, to
15th S/L Militia Depot RA
Oswestry

A further communication will be sent to you later.

Yours faithfully,

H. Jones
for.
Manager.

M.R. 88.

(4527) Wt. 17460-8851 60,000 6/39 T.S. 677

Call-up papers at the beginning of World War II in 1939. Elfed reported to Park Hall, Oswestry and was given the number 1533601, but was known as Davies 601 during the war.

Ready for war – Elfed in his Army uniform. The photograph was taken a few months after enlistment.

Bofors 40mm AA gun guarding the Rolls Royce Company works in Derby. At the time RR were producing Merlin engines for the Spitfire aeroplanes. Elfed in on the left. The balloon would be deployed to deter low level aircraft attacks.

On arrival in Egypt, July 1942. Elfed in third on the right in the back row. The first camp was set up at Geneifa, near the Suez Canal. Everyone is wearing drill shorts and Topi hats.

High jinks in the desert! Elfed is fourth from the right. The new arrivals acclimatised reasonably quickly to the dry heat and sun.

Lena (Helena) Davies was to become Elfed's wife. Lena served in the Women's Royal Air Force.

Elfed and Lena on their wedding day in April 1942. Soon after both had to return to their respective postings.

Newlyweds in uniform. Elfed wears the uniform of the Royal Electrical and Mechanical Engineers and Lena the uniform of the Women's Royal Air Force.

Fighting the war in Palmanova, Italy in 1945. Elfed is third from the left in the front row.

VE Day – 8 May 1945 in St Mark's Square, Venice. Time to do a little sightseeing on the journey north and home.

Elfed with his five sisters:
Megan, Beattie, Glenys,
Lizzie and Sal. Hannah Mary
had died young from TB.

A young family in post-war
Wales. Elfed and Lena with
their son Brian in 1946.

Nant-y-moch Farm and Blaenrheidol Chapel in 1960. Both were submerged by the development of the hydro-electric scheme reservoir in 1964. Two brothers, John and Jim James farmed here and looked after the chapel.

Elfed, Avril, Brian and Dad-cu Aberystwyth visiting John and Jim at Nant-y-moch. The brothers were always pleased to welcome visitors to their isolated home.

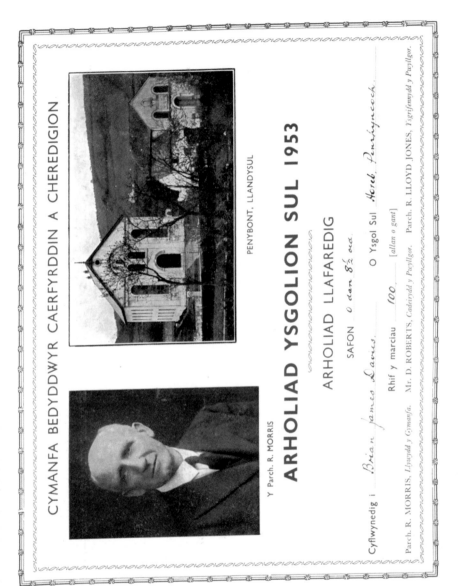

CYMANFA BEDYDDWYR CAERFYRDDIN A CHEREDIGION

PENYBONT, LLANDYSUL

Y Parch. R. MORRIS

ARHOLIAD YSGOLION SUL 1953

ARHOLIAD LLAFAREDIG

SAFON *0 dan 8½ oed.*

Cyflwynedig i *Brian James Lewis* O Ysgol Sul *Heol Penlbyncoch*

Rhif y marciau *100* [allan o gant]

Parch. R. MORRIS, *Llywydd y Gymanfa.*   Mr. D. ROBERTS, *Cadeirydd y Pwyllgor.*   Parch. R. LLOYD JONES, *Ysgrifennydd y Pwyllgor.*

Brian's Sunday school certificate from 1953. One hundred per cent pass mark
thanks to the endeavours of his teachers, David Jenkins and Sally Jenkins.

Brian about to be totally immersed for baptism in the Stewi stream at Penrhyn-coch in 1961. A large congregation witnessed the event from the riverbank.

looking west or north-west one night and seeing Coventry burning when it was blitzed.

I found the course very interesting, as it took in practical work such as soldering, the use of instruments and making up working models of receivers and transmitters from a selection of radio parts that the college held in its storeroom.

The reasons behind setting up the wireless mechanics course were now becoming obvious – the Navy already had a manual for wireless telegraphists and it was considered the bible on the subject by all the services. The RAF had a similar manual too. But the Army realised that radio communication was becoming more important and all armoured vehicles would be fitted with radios very soon. They didn't have the personnel trained for the maintenance of those, so it was decided to train extra men very quickly.

At the end of the course we were moved to Aldershot, billeted at Parsons Barracks on the outskirts and worked at the base workshops of the Royal Army Ordnance Corps (RAOC) nearby. This was a modern barrack and workshop, where we were introduced to the various radio sets and other equipment used in the Army at that time. Soon after, I was given a trade test, and on passing out as a Wireless Mechanic Grade III, I was no longer just a Gunner but a Private in the RAOC and given threepence a day extra in pay. The RAOC had two functions: firstly, the supply of most goods apart from rations to the Army and secondly, the repair and maintenance of such goods.

While on leave during my time at Aldershot, Lena and I got engaged. We'd been more than friends for years before the outbreak of war. She was due to do some form of National Service also.

There were many base workshops dotted all over the United Kingdom then: Stirling in Scotland, Mile Hill in London, Nottingham, and Belfast in Northern Ireland. Belfast served the whole province. A group of us were posted there in the autumn of 1941. We went by train to Heysham and sailed to Belfast during the night. This was not considered an overseas posting though, but it was close to it as we had to take the Full Service Marching Order (FSMO) with us which consisted of a rifle, bayonet, full set of webbing (belt and braces) including small pack and big pack, steel helmet and a gas mask, of course. Quite a lot to get on and off trains and a ferry with! When we arrived in Belfast, we were taken to the base workshop at Kinnegar, a few miles down the loch towards Bangor, County Down. It was a very modern workshop, located on the shore, though not quite finished at the time we arrived. Through its windows we watched the ships sailing in and out of the port of Belfast, and the arcs of the cranes building more ships in the distance.

Alongside the base at Kinnegar was the small town of Holywood, straddling the road between Belfast and Bangor. We ended up staying in a large empty house at the end of the town. Holywood was a nice little town with two small cinemas and various chapels. There were plenty of bus services to Belfast at all times.

In November I was given seven days leave and by then news came through that Lena had joined the Women's Auxiliary Air Force (WAAFs) and was doing her basic training in Blackpool. So my intention was to break my homeward journey there for a day or two and then make my way back to Salem. All was well until I realised that anyone going back to the mainland on leave had to take their FSMO kit also.

But it had to be done. So I travelled to Larne and sailed to Stranraer in Scotland and then caught a train down to Blackpool. As I needed to stay in Blackpool overnight, my concern was where to leave my clobber safely until the following morning. I managed to find a friendly police station sergeant who agreed to lock it up in a cell overnight. I met up with Lena in her new WAAF uniform, and the following day continued my journey to Aberystwyth.

A few days of leave was very pleasant and I started my long return journey to Belfast on the 1 p.m. train from Aberystwyth. The train in those days was full of service personnel. When

I reached the station I found that it was very crowded with very many waiting to board. I walked up and down trying to find an empty seat, and with my full kit on, that was no joke! I found myself in the middle of a wedding party, with the happy couple going away on honeymoon. I heard a voice shout my name: it was David Mason, Glanrafon, the father of the new bridegroom who had married Mary Penbanc that morning. They had reserved a compartment of the train and Dai Glanrafon ordered the porter to open the doors again and shoved me, with all my kit, into the compartment with the wedding party. It was probably the first time a honeymooning couple had left Aberystwyth with an armed escort, as far as Crewe anyway.

When I returned to Kinnegar I made the effort, as promised to Mrs Smith in Salem, to visit some members of her family, the Coopers, who lived at a place called Castlereagh on the outskirts of Belfast. I was invited to a party at their house a couple of days after Christmas 1941 and had a great welcome. Both Mr Cooper and his grown-up son worked in the city. My Christmas was pretty much the normal Christmas in the Army, when all the officers and non-commissioned officers served us at the table – a very old tradition, apparently.

Cinema visits were very important to us here too. One of the purpose-built cinemas in Holywood had a commissionaire/manager who would get very annoyed if someone in the audience made a dash for the door instead of standing rigidly to the playing of the national anthem 'God Save the Queen' at the end of the performance. The other cinema was once a two-floor terraced house: the top floor was removed and the ground floor became the cinema, with the operations box attached to the second-floor window and overhanging the pavement below. The poor operator had to access his box using a ladder from the outside pavement. Both cinemas provided good entertainment for us.

Early in 1942 came the news that most of us wireless mechanics and a large contingent of other tradesmen at the base were to be posted back to Aldershot on a new scheme. There we were billeted at Romiley Barracks in Farnborough where the Royal Aircraft Establishment (RAE) are still active to this day doing various experiments with British and foreign aeroplanes.

It soon became clear why we had gathered at Farnborough. There were now about 1,000 men of all ranks and trades at the barracks: fitters, mechanics, electricians, painters, blacksmiths and carpenters from the Royal Army Ordnance Corps (RAOC), Royal Army Service Corps (RASC) and the Royal Engineers. During the early campaigns in the Western Desert of Egypt and Libya, it had been apparent that the biggest deterrent to fast-moving armoured forces was the long distances that they had to operate from their base in the Suez Canal area. The armoured forces needed urgent repairs, maintenance and modifications done to equipment much nearer to the front line, rather than having to move hundreds of miles back to base camp for repairs and servicing.

The plan, therefore, was to form mobile workshops capable of doing most, if not all, of the work that had been done at the base workshop. These new workshops would be completely mobile and would need 250 to 300 men of all ranks to man it. The staff at Aldershot picked the cream of every trade from the 1,000 men gathered there to find the required personnel for these new units. After about five months there we were given another trade test and if passed we would become Tradesmen Grade II or I, and earn a few more pence each day in pay.

Those who failed the test were surplus to requirements and posted back to their former units. Those who passed became members of 323 Armoured Troops Workshop RAOC. The commanding officer was Lt. Col. Shields and a Major Carr was his deputy, Captain Smith was the Adjutant; he was a red-faced man of middle age and what he did not know about the Army was not worth knowing as he had been a soldier from the age of twelve and had served in every rank. We all had great respect for him. The unit also had a sergeant called Salter, a very smart man who was said to have been used by the Northern Command to show off various drill methods. He was a Sheffield bus driver by trade. I can still hear him in my mind shouting in his Yorkshire accent: "Where, there those men what hasn't had a bath?" on the parade ground!

In March 1942 I received a telegram saying that my father was very ill. I got compassionate leave at once and returned to Salem to find him with serious pneumonia – he died before the night was over. I made arrangements for the funeral at Salem after the post-mortem (compulsory for old miners) was held. Lena came home on leave as well and, after the funeral, we returned to our units knowing that the next leave would be our last for a while.

On my return to duty a new consignment of vehicles, all specially adapted to form a mobile workshop, had arrived. They were Leyland Retriever petrol-driven trucks with oil engines. They had six wheels, with the rear wheels in tandem so that a track could be fitted to them in soft terrain. This proved useful several times in the desert. Each vehicle had a letter such as an M Truck or D Truck, depending on whether it was a welder's, fitter's, or electrician's truck. The wireless mechanic's truck was the Z Wagon and was covered with a wire mesh to prevent radiation if testing a transmitter inside it. There was also a generator lorry, a cookhouse and a water wagon, and also office trucks – most with long, heavy cables to connect to the generator lorry to make us totally independent wherever we were sent.

Inside the Z Wagon was a range of electrical and radio instruments. There was also a small petrol generator so that we could be independent of the main supply if needed. The other wagons had lathes, milling machines, drills of all sizes, various welding sets and other equipment fitted into them. There were also one or two spare lorries to carry our kit when we were on the move. All in all it was like the Bertram Mills Circus! We even had a D8 bulldozer and Cole's crane.

Having gathered all our gear, we had yet more medicals

and inoculations to endure. Then we were all given seven days embarkation leave. I went home to Salem and by some good luck Lena got leave at the same time too. It was now early April 1942. We were destined to be married, so we decided, well why not then, before I went away; we could then draw a marriage allowance, which would come in handy when we would meet up again. As we only had a few days to arrange matters, it was all quite a rush. Tabernacle Chapel was chosen for the wedding which was officiated by the Rev. J Meredith. It was a quiet affair, in deference to my mother, who'd only been a widow for a month.

My biggest worry was finding a best man for the wedding ceremony on 14 April 1942 – all my old friends were away in the Services. However, my first cousin, David Benjamin or Dai Ben as he was popularly known, was available. So too Dei Jenkins, Lena's uncle. Dei was very tall and Dai Ben was short, so the photographer had his work cut out to have balance in the wedding photograph. The reception was held at Lena's home in Edge Hill Road. We stopped over for a one-night honeymoon in Shrewsbury and then made our way back to our units. I went to Aldershot and Lena to Oxford.

8

Departure Overseas and Convoy Life

AFTER MORE MEDICAL tests we were issued with tropical kit: the usual Khaki Drill (KD) slacks and what was then called Bermuda shorts; these were KD shorts with a very large turn-up, which we would be obliged to tuck into our hose tops to avoid being bitten by mosquitoes in certain parts of the world. There was also a Topi or a large sunhat. One advantage of my large hat was that nobody would take it by mistake, as it was far too big for anybody else's head. We were also issued with an extra kit bag known as Overseas Kit Bag White, which meant even more to carry!

When Lena and I met up briefly after the wedding, we thought of a code so that she'd know where I'd been posted overseas. I was to write "Hope Uncle Joe's leg is better" if I was destined for the Middle East. We had other codes for various ports of call, just in case. Pretty daft perhaps, but it worked and kept us informed with the latest news.

Drivers of all vehicles, over a hundred by now, left for the River Clyde in Scotland to be put aboard ship at the end of April 1942. The remainder of us, including all the officers, followed a few days later and boarded ship at Greenock and we sailed in convoy on 8 May 1942. There were a few American and other nationality's ships in our convoy which grew larger as we sailed out into the Atlantic. These American ships had brought their troops over to Northern Ireland. They had then come across the channel to pick us up. Our ship was the *SS Borinquen* of the Porto Rico Line. It sailed under the American flag, so the first thing we had to do after boarding was to change our money into American currency. It was quite amusing to handle dollars and dimes after each payday, though there was not a lot to spend it on. The keen card players had a field day, especially those who went to the crew's quarters to play, win or lose.

There were Spanish signs all over the ship: Senors, Hombres on various doors. We were twelve to a cabin and slept on steel bunk-beds in tiers of three, suspended by chains from the ceiling. We had to use the communal ablutions along the corridor and use sea-water soap to wash which we got used to in the end. We wore the minimum of clothes anyway, and finding somewhere cool to lie down was of greater priority to us. The food wasn't bad but rather monotonous. We had to make our own entertainment: a few lectures, plenty of bingo, or as we called it housey-housey.

An occasional long-distance plane would take a look at us now and again and then fly off, but we had no real threat to our safety as we zigzagged along the ocean. One amusing incident I remember: the Royal Horse Artillery (RHA) was on board with us and rather a snooty lot they were too. Instead of playing bingo on deck like all the other troops, they decided to practice their Morse code and brought out their field telephones which we, the workshop lads, were very familiar with. Each telephone had a buzzer which worked from an enclosed battery. They'd hardly sat down on deck when one of our escort destroyers on our flank could be seen coming full-on towards us and ordering the RHA to stop doing the Morse code practice at once. It seems that there were no wires attached to the field telephones, so the Morse signals were being picked up miles away from the solitude of the north Atlantic. That certainly put the RHA in its place!

We had a small dance band on board, made up of some of our Aldershot boys. One in particular, by the name of Cockran, was a very good instrumentalist. There were also pianists, drummers and a crooner. This all helped to pass the time of day. We had no newspapers but, an American by the name of Chaplain Parker, took it upon himself to go to the radio room and read us the news at 4 p.m. daily over the ship's PA system. This was the only news we heard of how the war was progressing. After about two weeks at sea, we sailed into Freetown, Sierra Leone in west Africa to refuel and water, and anchored offshore while little tenders shuttled back and forth to supply the whole convoy. Nobody was allowed ashore at all and we amused ourselves watching the tenders pumping the oil and water into our ship and the native crews diving over the side, although not swimming very far, as they were afraid of sharks.

Within a few days, however, the military police brought back one of our men whom they'd found ashore. It was Cockran, the musician, who had jumped overboard with his clothes wrapped in his gas cape strapped to his shoulders, and he had swam the mile or two to the shore, sharks or not, before being picked up by the military police. We didn't really admire his exploit; as a matter of fact we cursed him quietly as we had to, in turn, stand guard over him in solitary confinement at the bottom of the ship all the way to Suez. It wasn't a very pleasant job in the rough weather as we rounded the Cape of Good Hope.

A day or two after leaving Freetown there was great excitement – duck would be prepared for our evening meal. It transpired that the ship's catering officer had purchased a consignment of small ducks, enough for one between two, for the entire troop aboard. We had already learnt that on a troop ship of mixed regiments, the Army was always fed its personnel by seniority of regiment. The most senior regiment aboard the *Borinquen* was the RHA and they were the first to be served at each meal. This dish of duck contrasted a great deal to the never-ending stew that we'd had for the previous three weeks.

However, the RHA would also go up for a second helping, so by the time it was the turn of the poor RAOC, all the ducks had been eaten and there were none left. We never forgot that and many months later, while travelling in the Western Desert, we passed a convoy of the RHA and shouted at them in unison, "Who ate the ducks?" They knew what we meant and would laugh and carry on.

One evening, while still zigzagging our way down the south Atlantic, we passed fairly close by to the lonely island of St Helena – it was there that Napoléon had been exiled during the previous century. We saw lights ashore and wondered what life was like so far from anywhere? The weather through the tropics had been very warm and since we observed a strict blackout on board after sundown, the ship was like an oven inside, and it was very hard to get any sleep. A few of us, especially the non-smokers, slept on deck under the stars and would have to take a blanket up on deck early in order to secure a spot to sleep. Smoking on deck was totally forbidden, and those who could not endure being without a cigarette had to suffer in the stifling heat below deck.

We also had a rota for garbage duty; we would have to report to the galley in the bottom of the ship just before blackout time and be ready to throw all the rubbish that had accumulated during the day overboard. The convoy's commodore ship would give a siren signal at the appropriate time for all the rubbish to be tipped overboard. This was to avoid any U-boats finding the rubbish before it sank – they could follow and attack the convoy. We were learning fast about life at sea.

A few days later we saw the famous outline of Table Mountain on the horizon and knew that the first part of our journey was over. We entered Cape Town harbour and were directed to our various berths. As we docked there was a humorous incident. When each ship was in place the first man aboard was the Route Transportation Officer (RTO) to change all our money to South African Rand. This RTO's driver was a very attractive WAAF and she was standing on the quay. As all the men rushed to the starboard side of the ship to look at her, so the ship listed to the side of the quay. The captain became very annoyed and shouted to the officers to spread the men around the ship, so that she would float upright again. The sailors, of course, hadn't seen a woman for a month and so it was a bit of a novelty! The WAAF, fair play to her, sensed the problem and moved out of sight until the docking procedure was complete.

In Cape Town we were told that we'd have what was called 'hard lying', meaning sleeping in tents ashore. We were marched to the railway station with a pack and blanket each. Fortunately, our small arms remained in the ship's armoury. We were taken some twenty miles into the countryside to a tented camp called Retreat. This was a camp of bell tents of many a score in number, erected alongside a railway halt on sandy ground. As soon as we dumped our kit into the tents and had something to eat (mostly fresh fruit to make up for what we had missed for the last month), we returned to Cape Town on the next train.

It's hard to describe what Cape Town looked like in June 1942. Although it was their midwinter, it wasn't particularly cold but it did rain frequently. After two and a half years of blackout in the UK, with its rationing and other shortages, Cape Town seemed wonderful. All the shops and cinemas were lit up and there were plenty of goods in all the windows. It seemed as though you'd stepped back about three years in time in one fell swoop. We made our weary way back to the Retreat camp, many of us having taken the precaution of taking a groundsheet with us to cover our shoulders. We settled down to about six in a tent, with our feet touching the pole in the middle.

But, we awoke to find not a single tent standing. It seems that they were pegged into sand and nobody had bothered to slacken the guy ropes when the rain came – so they all collapsed. The order came to go back to the ship and there was a loud chorus of cheering. Each man recovered his blanket from the water and helped one another to wring it out. After breakfast we marched to the halt and boarded the train back to Cape Town.

When we emerged from the ship the following morning for our free day in Cape Town, there was a contingent of the South African equivalent of the Women's Voluntary Service waiting for us. They took us all to a nearby hall and, after refreshments, we were split into groups and taken by the ladies in their American Pontiac or Chevrolet cars to see the sights of Cape Town. We rode around all day before having tea in some out-of-town café. The same thing happened on the following days as well. Most of the boys loved buying the cheap watches as there was a huge choice that we had not seen in the UK for years.

We were amazed by the lifestyles of these WVS types – the one who drove us around had her very own private plane! Their homes were out of this world and like nothing I'd ever seen before. We also saw some good picture shows in their cinemas but, after five days of these wonderful experiences, it was time to go and pick up the rest of the convoy and head up the Indian Ocean.

An incident which has always remained in my mind occurred during this stage of the voyage. In the next bunk-bed next to mine was a fellow called Jack Berry who, in peacetime, had a radio shop in Redcliff on the outskirts of Manchester. He was an excellent craftsman and had worked himself up to Staff Sergeant, but had jumped one draft and been caught and demoted to craftsman. However, he knew all the tricks of the trade.

After leaving Cape Town we discovered that Jack had bought himself a rod and fishing line and was fishing in the sea from the stern of the ship. While we rounded the Cape of Good Hope, the weather was too rough to fish. It wasn't the sort of activity one would've imagined Jack taking a delight in, to be honest. However, there was a method in his madness. We learnt that the ship's purser had a strongroom in the hold for storing dollars to pay the passengers and crew during the voyage. Inside the strongroom were shelves stacked with hundreds of elasticated bundles of dollar bills. One morning the purser entered to find thousands of dollars on the floor, much like autumn leaves. It was obvious that someone had tried to fish out a few bundles and the elastic had snapped and the money had scattered on the floor. A quick check found that $3,000 were missing and so the search was on. The ship was far out at sea, so the culprit still had to be on board. Of course, Jack and his fishing tackle were the obvious suspects and the authorities turned over our cabin two or three times each day for weeks, but to no avail. Three thousand dollars was a lot of money in 1942, and the mystery was never solved and Jack was constantly asked: "What have you done with it?" at every turn, but we never found out!

We continued to zigzag our way up the Indian Ocean while listening each day to the chaplain's bulletin for news from the Western Desert, because it was there that we were destined for. Those ships going on to India had now left our convoy and we continued our way to Aden. It was June and very, very hot. We were concerned when we heard that British forces were retreating, and that Tobruk had fallen.

We anchored again to refuel and take on fresh water. It was here that we saw our Yankee crew panic and the incident made us feel grateful that we'd come this far without any serious problems. A tender was pumping oil into our ship when the fire bells went off and everybody dashed on deck to their appointed places, complete with life jacket and emergency ration pack etc. There was certainly smoke, but when we lined up on A deck we could see that it was coming from the funnel of the tender. Our crew were running around like mad and the captain on the bridge tried to give orders to them: "Run out your hoses on the starboard side of A deck," which they did. "Direct your hoses down the funnel of the ship," he again ordered. He meant, of course, the funnel of the tender, which would have been a very easy matter to deal with and would have solved the problem at once. Instead, they directed their hoses on the funnel of our own ship and the next thing we saw were our engineers dashing on deck using very uncomplimentary language as their engine room was flooded.

9

Egypt and the North Africa Campaign

IT WAS SOON time to be on the move once again. As a convoy we could not sail up the Red Sea. So, each ship set off up the Red Sea on its own, guarded by warships and planes from a distance. We passed numerous small islands and the desert loomed on either side. We heard on the news that the enemy had been halted at El Alamein in Egypt, and we were almost in Egypt ourselves now.

The order came for us to take our small arms from the armoury. At Suez we found that we would be ferried ashore by Arab tenders. Then we boarded a train with our kit and no sooner than the train pulled away we had our first taste of Egyptian life. We, as the train's new passengers were of huge interest to hordes of Arabs of all ages – it was like an infestation, each trying to sell us some sort of Egyptian souvenir, from wallets to silk scarves and fruits of all kind. We'd been warned beforehand that we were not to eat the fruit at all, which was, as some were to find out, a very good warning!

The train was packed and after leaving the outskirts of Suez, the Arab traders gave up. It was now getting dark and as soon as we were a few miles into the desert and not far from the Suez Canal, the train stopped and we were all ordered to disembark and move to some sand dunes not very far from the track. We were told to make ourselves comfortable there until we could return to the train sometime before dawn. We were not told why this was, but assumed that they were expecting an air raid on the train or the rail track. The enemy, who was not many miles away, had been aware of the arrival of a large convoy at the port. With nothing amiss we re-boarded the train at dawn, made our way to the Geneifa campsite not far from the Suez Canal. Alongside it was a PoW camp full of German soldiers, who jeered loudly as we marched past. Geneifa camp had a range of India Pattern tents with flysheets, a tented cookhouse and latrines dug deeply into the sand. A number of frontline troops were there already having a rest from their duties. The camp also had huge store sheds which were empty, where we would set up our workshops for a few weeks.

The main base workshops for the Egypt campaign were at a place called Telekabir, a few miles up the canal towards Cairo and the base at Geneifa was to be a substitute for that workshop. And it was there that we discovered that we were no longer the RAOC but the Royal Electrical and Mechanical Engineers (REME), the formation of which had been agreed upon while we were all at sea. We were no longer Privates but Craftsman so and so. Apart from having a new cap badge however, there was no difference.

Having been reunited with our vehicles, they were repainted to sand colour. We were also issued with two jeeps (the first we had ever seen) which proved very popular until the end of the war. The jeeps were commandeered by the Colonel and the Major who, like a couple of school boys, delighted in trying them out on the nearby sand dunes.

It was now the first week of July 1942 and the temperatures were very high. Fortunately, we worked inside the huge store sheds, which was more comfortable than being outside. Most of the workshop jobs were doing modifications, mostly welding extra water carrier brackets onto vehicles. The two most popular tanks at the time were the Crusader and Valentine, both lightly armoured with a small gun. The Crusader tank was also quite fast. The idea at the time was to try to get enough fuel to the battle zone and have enough to return to base. Extra fuel tank to be carried in a boot or on the engine cover had been invented, and these new designs could also be jettisoned off when empty by means of a cable operated by the driver. Our fitters spent many hours perfecting the device.

At work we had some PA equipment and a small amount of money in an entertainment fund. So we got our quartermaster to go to Cairo to buy a microphone and pick up some records. An old wind-up gramophone was converted to work off a car battery. So we had music while we worked. I remember that one of the records the quartermaster brought back from Cairo was Diana Durban singing 'There's No Place Like Home' – not a very intelligent choice for a bunch of men who'd recently arrived in Egypt. We soon sorted that out by drilling another hole off-centre in the record and then playing it again. It sounded more like the Mohammedian call to prayer, which amused everyone apart from the quartermaster himself.

During August new tanks for the armoured troops arrived. These were the first Sherman tanks and sent directly from America. They were just what the British armoured troops needed. But, the trouble was that the Yanks had not put a suitable engine in them and had to substitute an aero-radial engine to drive them. This was all very well except that they had to have 100-octane fuel to work them, which meant more petrol had to be moved to the desert. A special drill also had to be learnt when starting the engines up. If someone happened to stop by just switching off the engine, the high octane petrol in the system would collect at the top of the bottom cylinder, and when next switched on, a flame of 30 feet would shoot out of the exhaust, to the peril of anyone or anything standing nearby.

Like all aero-engines it was necessary to have them serviced every 100 hours of running time. A clock on the dashboard would tell when it was time for a service. A concern for us wireless mechanics was the fact that these Sherman tanks were all fitted with FM radios, but there were no FM radios in use in those days in the British Army. Therefore all radios had to be ripped out and replaced by the faithful No.19 radio set. This was a well-tested set and could be adapted for use anywhere by means of various control boxes. Some were even made in America under the Lend/Lease agreements; they were also issued to Russian troops and were fitted in some aeroplanes. The only other radio sets we came across in our work were back-carrying infantry sets, mostly worked by dry batteries.

An Australian character called Shafto built a series of open-air cinemas at various points in Egypt. These cinemas were just four walls built around a square, with seats in the middle, a screen at one end and an operating box at the other, but no roof. Films could only be seen after dark and he would also supply some refreshments, mostly bread rolls with a fried egg.

Shafto employed some Arab youngsters to operate these makeshift cinemas; they often got reels of film mixed up and the villain, although shot, would be alive again before the end of the film! The Aussies in the audience would make their way to the operator's box and give him a good hiding for his mistake. These cinemas were known as Shafto's Shufties.

Later we were issued with a bivouac, a small two-man tent, so we knew we were destined to move 'up the blue' as moving into the desert was known. So we travelled through Cairo and onto a place called Maryopolis, not far from Alexandria. We camped in those small tents on a sand hill in the desert. We didn't set up workshops there – as we guessed that something very big was going to happen soon. While waiting we were given time off in Alexandria and the evenings were spent at the local Shafto in the desert. After darkness fell, it was difficult to find our way back to the camp, and more than one of us just slept on the sand waiting until daylight, before returning to camp. Eventually a small light bulb was placed on top of a flagpole to help us find our way back to camp.

Some of the Arabs would steal anything from us. Sleeping in those small tents, we soon found out that anything you left outside would be gone by morning, and it was also known for a hand to come in during the night and even take the blanket covering you. I lost a lot of kit including a pair of shoes in this way. We learnt quickly, once again.

On the night before the battle of El Alamein, two Army HQ padres visited us from Army HQ for a communion service in the open air. It has stuck in my mind ever since. We were just out of shelling range but, at about 10 p.m., the famous Eighth Army barrage started. The sky to the west looked as if it was on fire and the noise was the continuous rumble of thunder. The desert Air Force continued with the bombardment for several days and nights. The news on the radio told us that the Germans were in retreat, so we knew that General Montgomery had done it. But many old hands kept saying that they'd seen all this before and that the Germans would just wait a while. The desert Air Force were flying back and forth all day, hammering the retreating forces, and soon came the news that we were also to move up the line, as there was plenty of work to do now.

Our main concern was defence against an air attack – we couldn't hide an outfit like ours no matter how good the camouflage was. So, the only answer was dispersal: any congregating of men or vehicles was disapproved of. So a plan was drawn up. It was important that the wagons of the machine shop section, including our Z wagons which would require an electrical supply to operate them, would be within a reasonable distance of a generator. But men such as welders were mobile and could work anywhere. Then there was the question of keeping the workforce fed, and it was decided that there would be three or four feeding points, and that a truck from the cookhouse would visit each point three times a day, bringing rations to us in heat-retaining containers. Sometimes it would be several days before we would see or talk to friends from another feeding point. The theory was that no enemy plane would bother to attack a solitary truck or man in such a vast area. The system worked well and, we were not raided at all. Further into the desert there were two or three attempts to drop anti-personnel bombs on us during the night. These were what we called 'thermos' bombs as they were dropped more than half a mile away and would only explode as the sun rose and heated them. They made a very loud crack, usually when we were having breakfast.

We were taught how important it was to sleep below the level of the ground at night in case anything was dropped on us. Therefore, with each move, the first job was to dig a hole in the hard sandstone, about four or five feet deep and about three feet wide, usually long enough for two to sleep head to head. The hole would then be covered with two bivouacs, again end to end. The sandstone was very hard but we could carve into it to make nooks and crannies to keep various things in the tent. The tent would be lit by a car battery, as there were plenty of those around from abandoned vehicles. When the battery ran down we would take it to the staff electrician to be charged again. We had to ensure that no light was showing at night. It could get quite chilly about an hour before dawn, but as soon as the sun was up it became very warm.

We were impressed with the vast array of war machinery which had been destroyed during the recent battle – hundreds upon hundreds of all kinds of vehicles were scattered in every direction, especially along the coast road, apparently destroyed by our planes while trying to make a run for it.

We set up our first workshop near Messa Matuk, but quite soon we moved up the line again in convoy, between fifty to a hundred miles each time. The most precious commodity in the desert was water, far more so than petrol. Petrol was sourced from somewhere in Palestine, in oblong four-gallon tins with a cardboard sleeve around them. They were very poorly made and leakages were frequent. While on the move we would pull into a petrol dump to refuel, but had to be vigilant before pouring any petrol into our tanks to ensure that it was really petrol and not water. The amount of sabotage down the line was also immense. Although the containers were very poor for transporting petrol, they were very useful for other things such as making tea! One would get an empty petrol tin, cut it in half with a can opener and make a wire handle for each half to hang on the towing hook of the truck. Then, one half would be filled with sand and be soaked with petrol. The other half would be filled with water and put on top of the first half after setting light to the petrol. When it came to the boil, in went the tea leaves. Another tip we learnt was that a matchstick floating on the water would take away any taste of smoke that the tea might have had. When in convoy (which could be anything over a mile long), and the order for a rest would come, within a matter of minutes one would see a string of fires being lit as each vehicle got its own brew going before it was time to move on again.

The Germans had a different means of transporting petrol: by way of a jerrycan, which is still in use today. The Yanks copied the jerrycans eventually and made them for us as a result of the Lend/Lease agreement.

Once the Eighth Army started to move again, a directive came that any spare transport capacity was to be used to carry anything going westwards. All the broken vehicles scattered all over the desert were made into trailers. We then had more vehicles to carry petrol, water, tyres, spare parts or anything that was going to the west.

Water was the most important resource, and the enemy sabotaged many deep wells during their retreat. It meant that water had to be carried fifty to a hundred miles or more and it was strictly rationed. The coast road was not far from the sea, and many of us had a dip during the winter to keep ourselves clean. There were no fixed toilet facilities, so when the call of nature came one would pick up a shovel, some toilet paper, choose a direction and take a walk. The officers would do likewise, but would drive a jeep – so their chosen spot was further away.

In the desert there wasn't much wildlife to be seen. There was talk that there were desert foxes around, but I didn't see one. Rommel, the German Africa Corps Commander, had adopted the name to describe himself, signifying an elusive character. However, the elusive character that we did come across in those days was Popski. He was the Commander of a very selective band of soldiers known to all as Popski's Private Army. Reports at the time indicated that he was an Eastern European, probably Russian. He had gathered together a lot of desperados and the Army had been authorised to give them any help they might need – some used to say on Winston Churchill's instructions even.

They had a few vehicles, mainly jeeps, to move around the desert and they visited our workshops many times for minor repairs or welding jobs. One good look at some of their vehicles more than justified the name given to the group as each vehicle was loaded down with every type of weapon that could be carried: from mortars to flame throwers and guns of every description. Their main purpose was to harass the enemy wherever it could be found, often miles behind the lines – then Popski's men would disappear. They also had authority to pick up food and ammunition. We were instructed to help them in any way we could. What happened to them in the end I never managed to find out, but I certainly wouldn't like to have been on the wrong side of them. I never heard of them working on the mainland of Europe at all. Perhaps they were just desert nomads.

After setting up our workshops and digging foxholes, the next thing to do was forage around for what we could find, often on sites that the enemy had once occupied. We had to be extra careful in this, as there were still many landmines and vehicles which had been booby-trapped. It makes me shudder now to think of the risks we once took to look for pieces of wood or iron to make a camp bed.

We found nearly a dozen field telephones and a ten-line switchboard that our infantry had left behind in their hurry to advance. We also found many miles of field telephone wire which had been gathered and wound onto large drums.

As we approached Tobruk, we came across a German Air Force camp and found a great deal of photographic material: pieces of film, fixing lotions, enlargers etc. When we reached Benghazi's telephone exchange we discovered a number of reels of enamelled copper wire of all gauges which would prove to be useful to our many model- and gadget-makers later. We also found the remnants of an old civilian radio receiver which we modified to our purposes. Loudspeakers at the time were in very short supply, but adapting headphones used in tank by enlarging its cone and suspending it in an aluminium frame, could work well in a small tent at night. We would lay a line of old telephone wire among the other tents and soon there would be a dozen home-made speakers connected to it. Some of these would be very crude affairs, probably made by a blacksmith or a welder and we would have to put a limit on the number connected as there was hardly enough power coming out of the old set to work them all. It was great entertainment during the long hours of darkness.

In Benghazi we were billeted at the Italian Barracks of the motorized units. There were a few attempts to bomb us out, but to no avail. Then we travelled south following the coast road to a place called Adjedabia, a very desolate place. There was some concern about this place, as the British Army had pushed the enemy back as far as here on more than one occasion, before having to retreat. Our lines of communication were now at full stretch. Christmas 1942 was upon us and we spent it pretty miserably in fairly bad weather: high winds and a few showers of hail.

We were soon ordered to move west again. Tripoli was our first goal, and we stopped and set up shop at a place called Siste. (From recent maps I saw that [the late] Colonel Gadaffi had a few oil wells in operation there.) We worked very hard, working from dawn until dusk. As we neared Tripoli, the capital of Libya, we could see the relics of Mussolini's great dream of an Italian empire in North Africa. A lot of emigrants from Italy had been granted a small plot of land in the desert, not very far from the coast. They'd fenced or built a wall around a patch of ground, sank a deep well with a windmill pump to source water which would flow into a holding reservoir, with a series of ducts to water their plants, such as tomatoes and cucumbers. The little houses were very spartan, built of reinforced concrete and painted pink with Mussolini's slogans in large letters on the walls, such as: Credere, Obidere, Combattere (to believe, to obey, to fight). Many of these settlers had come from the slums of Naples; they must have thought they were in heaven.

In early spring 1943 we passed the town of Misurata and then entered the outskirts of Tripoli itself. It was quite a change for us to see a few civilians walking about as the Eighth Army had been through and were now chasing the enemy towards Tunisia.

Not long before the North African Campaign, a unit known as the Long Range Desert Group was operating in the Western Desert. These were mainly men from crack regiments of the British Army's Guards' Brigades. Some had been in the Middle East for many years, and had made an intensive study of the desert water wells and tracks. They worked miles behind enemy lines during the various combats. They moved small convoys up and down the desert, laying fuel dumps and emergency food and water in certain places. They were well known to many storytellers, who have since revealed that they picked up the various stragglers who had either been shot down or crashed or lost in the desert.

During our workshop's push up the desert we came into contact with members of this famous group. They had armoured cars with powerful radios and reported most enemy traffic movements daily or nightly back to their superiors in Cairo. When they needed repairs, such as a service or modifications done to their vehicles, they were directed to us. We would weld brackets to the sides of their armoured cars to carry more water and fuel cans. When this work was being done they would camp with us, and many a late evening was spent listening to tales of their exploits. They were a very rare breed indeed and, having been out in the Middle East for so long, they could speak Arabic and that would fool the nomadic Bedouin tribes that wandered the desert, as they wore Arab dress too.

By now we'd moved into Tunisia and knew that before we could go much further west, there would be a formidable obstacle in front of us – the heavily fortified Mareth line. This was Rommel's final line of defence – the German Afrika Corps had made a final last stand on their retreat west here. By now also there was news that the British First Army had landed in Algiers, and was progressing towards us. However, the most significant news to us was the advance of the Long Range Desert Group to the south of the Mardeth line. This had resulted in them finding a possible way around the southern end of the line, deep in the desert and was enough for Monty to try again his now-famous left hook.

We were kept busy at a place called Ben Gardane adapting vehicles making this long trip around the fortified line. We were warned that, should the enemy make a bolt back towards us, we were to stay where we were, as we had some armour in the workshop which might frighten them off.

Monty's tactic worked and soon the enemy was heading for Tunis. We never got to Tunis, but were confined slightly to the south. The ground at our camp there was very hard to dig our sleeping foxholes. We wandered around some Arab villages selling figs which grew nearby for eggs. Arabs in the desert were always keen to buy tea leaves and there was no fooling them if anybody tried the old trick of drying used tea leaves and passing them on. Apparently, they used to brew tea to make some form of a much sought-after drug.

Mail from home took a long time to arrive in the Middle East – often two or three months perhaps. Although my mother used to send me the *Cambrian News* every week, two or three would often come at the same time, with news of who had been home on leave and who had got married etc.

Another means of communication was developed by the Services during the war. It was called the airgraph. We would buy an A4-size airgraph sheet, write on it and hand it in paying a few pence postage. This would then go to a central point such as Army HQ; it was then photographed onto film and flown to London, developed, enlarged and posted on. The same thing would happen in reverse in Britain. The system worked very well and reduced the transit time of news to loved ones. But they were censored before being sent.

Another method of communication was the green envelope whereby we would be issued with a green envelope and sign a declaration on the back that its contents did not include anything of benefit to the enemy. These were also subject to censorship at Army HQ and the penalty for false declaration was very severe.

As mentioned earlier, the Sherman tanks of the Eighth Army had high octane petrol engines at this time and it was only on the Tunisian border that we encountered the first Sherman tanks fitted with diesel engines. These were tanks that the Yanks had brought to North Africa or had been captured from the Germans by the British. These tanks had something which our boys were not used to dealing with – fuel injectors and pumps which, in the harsh environment of the Western Desert, would require specialist servicing techniques and facilities.

News filtered through that the Italians, who were well in advance of Britain in developing diesel equipment, had subsequently launched a special vehicle to service diesel parts and had been using it in the desert. We needed to get hold of one. We knew from reports that most of the Africa Corps were now cornered in the peninsula of Cape Bon in northern Tunisia, and that those not taken prisoner were making their way across the Mediterranean Sea in the same way that we had evacuated Dunkirk three years earlier. At Cape Bon, therefore, there were hundreds of German and Italian vehicles abandoned after their occupants had made their getaway. Our commanding officer dispatched our staff sergeant instrumental mechanic with a driver to forage around Cape Bon for the servicing vehicle that they were looking for. They returned a few days later with the Fiat vehicle, but both men had bandaged heads. The first vehicle they had found was booby-trapped and blew up (hence the injuries), but they found another one and brought it back. It was a small 30-seater bus, stripped out and lined inside with aluminium. It was fitted with its own power supply, sinks, pumps, benches and all the instruments required for the job in hand. The commanding officer was overjoyed, and the men's injuries were soon better. One trouble problem with all the Fiats however was that the silencer was noisy and the vehicle could not be adapted to use a British or American one.

We were now just south of Tunis and the order came for us to return to the outskirts of Tripoli. We turned east and bypassed both Sousse and Sfax and retraced our steps to Tripoli which was still held by the enemy, the Italians, as part of their envisaged empire. We set up workshops just off the road that led from Tripoli to Castel Benito airport. Alongside our camp were the immigrant homes, with windmill pumps and 25-foot square reservoirs. One of the windmills was broken, so a bargain was struck between our fitters and the owner. If they'd repair it we could all enjoy a cold dip in the reservoir everyday before irrigation of the vegetable plot. The bargain was struck! They were stifling hot days in the summer of 1943, without a breath of wind until late afternoon when a strong breeze would come from the south-west, enough to turn the windmill to pump water into the reservoir. After 6 p.m., the wind would die down and the farmer would open the sluices and let the water out to irrigate his plot. Very many naked Royal Electricians and Mechanical Engineers would have gratefully splashed about by then! The water must have been drawn from a very deep well below ground as it was ice cold when it surfaced.

Not far away from us the Americans had set up their field

hospital. All our sick personnel were referred there, only to come back with a shirt pocket-full of aspirin, the Yanks' universal remedy for all complaints from desert sores to headache. On their return our own medical orderly would ask each patient to tip out his pockets into a large bowl. They must have been bringing them by the barrelful from America!

Our dance band and concert party was revived again and performed on a makeshift stage in camp. They were even invited to other units and transit camps to perform. I usually accompanied them on the excuse that I helped set up the PA system. In Tripoli itself there was a very nice theatre called the Royal Miramare, situated just behind the promenade and we performed there once or twice.

One thing I always recall from Tripoli. After leaving Egypt we'd continued to use Egyptian money (not that we needed much money in the desert anyway). Now 1,000 miles from Egypt, we could use money again, if only to buy ice cream from the Italian population. The Services decided to print its own money, sterling, as the Italian lira was the enemy's money up until then. We were paid in Allied Military Government currency in paper money – pound and shilling notes.

The director of Royal Electricians and Mechanical Engineers service of the Eighth Army amalgamated all the workshop units together under his overall command. We then started preparing all vehicles for landing on beaches. Then came the time for all the vehicles to gather at Tripoli dock to be loaded aboard landing craft. For over a week I was used as a temporary electrician. We had to check every vehicle before it drove onto the landing craft to make sure its starter worked perfectly. We had a tin of thick grease to smother on top of each battery, and a lot of condoms were used to slip over each filter cap, having first pierced it with wire so that the battery gas could escape and water would not enter the acid.

One day, when loading Landing Ship Tanks (LST) with vehicles, guns and a considerable amount of ammunition, one of them got into difficulty: the smoke generator tipped and the oil poured onto ammunition below – the flame from the smoke generator lit the whole lot. I remember diving beneath a Bedford truck when this happened and looking on cautiously as boxes of ammunition exploded and flew through the air. Guy Fawkes Night had nothing on this! The hatch cover of the LST was later found on the roof of the Royal Miramare Theatre in town. One naval officer was killed in the incident. But it was a very secretive time, and there was no further mention of the explosion anywhere. It certainly shook those of us who were working there.

We saw the crews of the LSTs off and wished them well knowing that we would be following them soon. We listened to news of the Salerno landings on mainland Italy. But we were ordered back to Egypt first for some leave, before departing again for the front. It took us several days to travel the 1,000 miles back to the Nile delta, retracing the coast road.

It was a long drive to Egypt and we arrived back at almost the same place where we'd started a year earlier: America, a few miles to the west of Alexandria. The Army had vetted a few pensions, which is what they called the B&B places, for us to sleep and eat. Those Arab-run houses were very good, clean and comfortable with proper beds which were a pleasant change. We enjoyed the sights of Alex, though few of us had the courage to walk alone through the native quarter. We got back to camp at the end of four days' leave to find that our new commanding officer hadn't taken his leave. I was nominated to drive him and a recently-appointed major to Alexandria for a night out at the Cecil Hotel on the seashore. The commanding officer was driven in an American-style Ford Station Wagon. I was given instructions to collect him at 11 p.m. and to bring a friend as company, because we had to drive through some very unpleasant areas on the way. I had difficulty finding someone to come with me, but all turned out well in the end. And so came to an end my time in North Africa.

10

Across the Mediterranean to Italy

AFTER OUR PERIOD of leave we were ordered to park all vehicles by some sand dunes ready for departure back to Europe. I was asked to take the commanding officer's car. All other non-drivers boarded a ship at Alexandria docks. We had to await another ship, so we spent the time playing football in the sand. We slept in our vehicles, yet passed the time very pleasantly.

We were eventually ordered to Alexandria's docks and were loaded by crane onto a cargo ship. We were now part of the Fourth Armoured Brigade of the Second New Zealand Division under General Fryberg or 'Tiny' to all his men. I remained with them until the end of the war.

We slept on the deck during the voyage and the Kiwis set up a cookhouse on to feed us. Reminding us that the war was not yet over each ship, as it left harbour, had to fire a single shot at a target moored about a mile away to test its gun on the stern end of the ship. We sailed across the Mediterranean Sea and anchored in August 1943 in eastern Sicily to refuel. Then we sailed around the heel of Italy and docked at Bari harbour in the south-east of the country. While the CO's car was being unloaded, there was a mishap with a crane – damage was done to the car's rear spring. There were a few fitters amongst the

Kiwis and it was agreed that they would fix it immediately as they wanted everyone away from the port as soon as possible as there might be an overnight air raid. All vehicles were parked that night close to Bari football stadium. The air raid continued all night with the anti-aircraft putting on quite a show. As waves of planes came overhead we would leave our vehicles and find shelter near a concrete stadium. Sheltering with us were many civilians, together with their animals. All in all it was quite terrifying; we could hear the shrapnel from our guns pinging off the concrete stadium above our heads.

At dawn we found a war correspondent who'd been sleeping next to me in his pick-up dead. He had a long sliver of steel shrapnel through his chest, it had come through the canvas roof of his vehicle as he slept.

After a minor repair job on the car, I then went up the coast to find my unit which was encamped at a place called San Severo, a little beyond Foggia. The unit were using bivouacs as it was pouring with rain. The roof of my car was now showing just how long it had been in the desert, and was leaking like a sieve. I laid my gas cape over my blanket and slept in the car again that night.

I found my mates in the morning, but it was still continuing to rain. I bedded down in my bivouac but, before too long, I had a corker of a dose of tonsillitis. The Army must have anticipated this illness as we were all going down like flies with exactly the same thing. They arranged for those suffering to be transferred to two large empty houses in the town of San Severo, to be under the care of a medical officer and RAOC orderlies for a few days. It wasn't surprising that we'd fallen ill, having come from the warmth of Egypt to sleep in bivouacs in Italy.

I was placed in a spartan room on a stretcher-type bed for two or three days – I soon felt better again and was able to rejoin the unit. On my return I found that we'd been issued with what were called 180-pounder Indian type tents with fly sheets instead of the old bivouacs. These could sleep six men very well, even with home-made stretcher-type beds. At least we were now off the wet ground and our health would improve.

We moved on to a place called Lanciano and took over a disused railway station on the Adriatic line. Trains weren't running then and we used the booking office as a wireless workshop and the waiting room as our dormitory. The fitters set up their workshops in the railway station's yard; it was ideal hard ground for the job. We could still hear the artillery of both sides banging away over the hills each night.

Our next move was to not such a pleasant place. It was the bank of the River Sangro, and it was there that we spent Christmas 1943 in deep mud and continuous rain. We had a Christmas dinner of some sort in our mess tins. Regarding sleeping arrangements, and so as to make more room in our tent which was pitched in a nearby field, I managed to get my bed into the cab of a Leyland stores wagon and put a spare flysheet over the canvas cab of the wagon to keep the warmth in. A friend of mine, Sergeant Ken Daley slept in a hammock between store bins in the back of the truck. Nights were incredibly long, as it went dark so early.

On New Year's Eve it snowed all night and in the morning Ken Daley and I were asked to go to the field to dig out the rest of our gang whose tent had collapsed because of the weight of snow. We dug them out and managed to repair the tent, but it was bitterly cold and not a very nice welcome to the new year of 1944.

We then heard on the news that the Army's advance up the west coast of Italy towards Rome had been halted – the fortified Monte Cassino had held them up and there was no way around it. It was fairly close to Route 6, the main road towards Rome, and it had to be overcome. There had been several battles already and the New Zealanders were ordered to help. And as we were a part of their company we had to go as well.

We set off in a large convoy over the top of the Apennine mountains. There was an ice field at the highest point of the mountain and a D8 bulldozer was stationed there to help all the traffic over the peak. Several vehicles would be hitched together and the D8 would tow them over the summit and let them make their own way down the other side. The theory of this operation was fine but we had more than our quota of home-made trailers, most without overrunning brakes. Therefore we had a few scary minutes descending that mountain. It was very cold up there, but the views were superb.

We descended into the valley and pulled into a coppice for the night – we ate our evening meal and bedded down in our vehicles. But something rather amusing happened overnight; a unit of American troops had pulled back from the front line with orders to return to the place where they'd started from, which was the spot we'd now inadvertently occupied. It gave us a taste of the Yanks' thinking as, instead of camping to the right or left of us, where there was plenty of room, they moved in amongst us! When we rose in the morning we could hardly move for American trucks which were in every nook and cranny between our wagons. We could hardly believe it!

After breakfast we moved a few miles up the road and camped in a field just out of shelling range of Monte Cassino itself. We could see the battle on the skyline, with the Casualty Clearing Station (CCS) located about a mile behind us. A few days later I visited it so that I could have a tooth removed.

The field chosen to set up our workshop was a little too soft for heavy armoured vehicles to traverse. So, for the first few days we all had to carry stone from a local quarry which the Yanks had reopened. We loaded lorries and then spread the stone to make a road around our workshop. We experienced how keen the Yanks were to use explosives: they used Teller mines to cut the stone. We worked hard and once the job was complete we were all given a day off to visit Naples and Pompeii, some thirty miles away. We travelled by lorry with twenty to twenty-five of us in the back of each lorry. Just before our daytrip to Vesuvius, it had erupted violently and we could see the results from our camp over twenty miles away. This eruption was the last in the twentieth century and on our day off we could see ash lying everywhere. The volcano quietened down quite quickly and it certainly was worth seeing the old houses of Pompeii, which were over two thousand years old.

Fortunately we were given four more days of leave in Salerno, a nice seaside town on the Gulf of Naples. We stayed in an Army camp and enjoyed the break as the weather had much improved by then. The coastline was very beautiful. Not long after our arrival back at camp, news came that a final push on Monte Cassino had started, with the New Zealanders and Poles having an important role. Up until then the Allies had been reluctant to bomb the old monastery, but on this particular morning we saw a plane from our side bombing the site. The Germans surrendered Monte Cassino and in a few days the Kiwis moved up the line, followed by us. We stayed in a village in the next valley called Isola del Liri. We were billeted in an old paper mill and could hear the Guards Brigade chase after the Germans who, by agreement, had bypassed Rome and fled north. The local Italians were very pleased to see all the Germans go as they had given them a hard time, especially since the native force had come over to the Allies during the war.

We experienced this one evening in Isola. My friend Reg Simms and I went for a walk around the village after our meal and some of the locals would come and chat to us over a glass of wine. A young lad of about twelve came up to us and begged for a tin of corned beef for the following day, as the locals were all living on meagre rations. We asked why it was so important to eat some meat. The lad explained that he was in training to be an opera singer, but since the Germans had invaded that had had to stop. They'd hidden his piano in a cave in the woods, just in case Jerry would have stolen it.

Now that the *soldati inglesi* had arrived, it was time to get the piano out again, such was their faith in us. There was to be a grand party the following day on the reappearance of the piano and to help the celebrations there was nothing better than a tin of Bully Beef. Reg and I knew that if we looked through the tanks in the repair workshops we would find a few rations somewhere. We made a deal with the young lad that if he returned to the bridge the following day and gave us a song, we would find him a tin of Bully. We all turned up at the right time and lifted him up to the parapet of the bridge on what was a lovely summer's evening and he sang for us the famous aria from Tosca – 'When the stars were brightly shining'. My mind often goes back to that evening on the bridge in Isola del Liri and I wonder what happened to that little lad and that tin of Bully.

At about the time of the fall of Monte Cassino, news came through of the Normandy Invasion and D-Day, and it made us all feel that it would not be long now before the end of the war. We moved on to the north of Rome, to a place called Sienna, famous for its horse racing around the town square. We didn't stop there very long as we were ordered to make our way towards the Adriatic coast once more. We went through Perugia and on to Assisi in convoy, and we stopped there a while. I remembered that Ifor, my childhood friend, was stationed there, so I went to look for him. I found him with a field ambulance unit. We didn't have much time together, as I had to move on towards the coast again.

After a few more stops, we reached the seaside town of Pesaro, and set up workshops in some buildings which had once belonged to the Italian Army. As winter was nearly upon us, we were billeted to sleep in some houses in Strada Pantano. Five of us wireless mechanics shared a room with a family called Batchocci. Senora Batchocci was a widow – her husband had been the local station master but had been killed in an air raid. She had two sons and two daughters aged from 14 to 22. We lived with them until April 1945. This was a typical Italian house: no carpets but stone floors everywhere. The welcome during that winter was wonderful and we shared their fire after we'd repaired the flue on their stove which had been damaged by the Germans.

We spent many hours with the youngsters. They began to learn a little English and we a little more Italian. We listened to the news as to how the war was going in France and Germany. The fighting on our side of the Italian frontier was very quiet then as things were bogged down up the coast near Rimini. Some of the Eighth Army's most famous divisions like the 51st Highlanders, the 7th Armoured and the 78th had been sent to Normandy, so what was left of the Eighth Army in Italy was now a mixture of all nationalities: Poles, Indians and South Africans – even our famous General Monty had long gone.

Christmas 1944 came and went and we celebrated this one in a marquee at the camp. For entertainment we would go to the town of Pesaro where there was an opera house which staged a number of Entertainments National Service Association (ENSA) shows for us. Pesaro was the birthplace of the composer Rossini and a famous musical academy was built in his memory there. We saw an opera there once or twice too.

When I had four days of leave my friend Reg Simms and I spent it in Florence. Later we were offered a day out in San Marino, a state within a state. San Marino had its own government, Army and police and was a very quaint little town. The day of our visit, Easter Sunday 1945, meant that everyone was walking around in their Sunday best as Easter Sunday was, and still is, an extra special day to the Italians.

When Senora Batchocci heard that I was to visit San Marino, she asked me to do her a favour. She had a brother living there; he was the local veterinary surgeon and she owed him some money. When I asked her how I was to find him, she said there was no problem – I was to go to the main bar in the town around midday and shout "Signor Batchoci, Doctore Animale" and he would soon come! I don't know how much money I had in the envelope, but we found him and duly followed to his practice. He was very grateful as he had not seen his sister since the Germans' arrival. There was little to show that San Marino was war damaged that Easter Day. It seemed as though the whole place was full of marching bands parading and a good time was had by all, despite the front line not being that far away.

By the time we returned to Pesaro it was obvious that the war was coming to an end. We were ordered to move up the coast towards Rimini, but there was one more job that needed to be done. Our company pulled in just off the beach near Cattolica, and about six or eight of us were ordered on a scouting operation. We and our kit were taken to a little village up in the hills and we were billeted in the local school. We soon found out what our secret job was. In a field near the village, tucked secretly under the hedges, were half dozen or more old Valentine tanks belonging to the Guards' Brigade. These had been adapted by means of a kind of 'skirt' around their base, which was raised and lowered by hydraulics which meant that they could float across a river when the 'skirt' was raised. We were asked to move the radio and aerial to the other side of the turret to allow the hydraulics to work better. It took us a couple of days or so to do the job and intelligence told us to move the tanks and cross the River Po slightly to the north. It was supposed that as soon as the Germans knew that armour had crossed the Po (although it was only Valentine tanks), Germany would surrender and the Italian Campaign would be over.

Job done, we returned to our unit and moved towards Bologna. The yard of a fruit canning factory on the outskirts became our new home. We dispersed into a nearby field while waiting for infantry to clear any snipers which had been left behind as the Germans retreated. I shall always remember that while we were waiting a farmer started digging furiously in the middle of the field. As he dug we were shocked to see the exhaust of a tractor coming to view! Yes, he had buried his valued tractor completely in the field so that the Germans would not take it. Soon the tractor was mobile again and we were also ready to move on.

We headed for Venice and, by the time we reached Mestre on the Venetian causeway, VE Day was underway and, although we heard on the radio of great celebrations in the UK and elsewhere, it was very quiet with us.

Our next destination was Trieste, which stands on the border of Italy, Yugoslavia and Austria. All three of these countries had occupied Trieste at some point. For a good while there had been an uneasy peace as it had been occupied by the Yugoslavians under Marshall Tito and also the Italians. The Allies were moving as many troops as possible into the surrounding area to help keep the peace. We were based on the coast near Monfalcone, some twenty miles from Trieste, in an area that belonged to a shipbuilding company which had quite a few large sheds and timber-drying barns on the site. But there was no electricity. However, there was plenty of room to set up workshops. A small stream ran through the site, so an open-air cold shower was soon erected alongside this.

We had a new commanding officer in charge by now, a man called Colonel Whiteley. While many other Army units stationed around us were having half-days down on the beach every day almost, we had to work just as hard as we had done during the war, on the excuse that our armour vehicles etc. would be needed for the Far East Campaign soon.

We were informed that a padre from Army HQ would be visiting us one Sunday morning to hold a thanksgiving service for winning the war. The service was held in an empty large shed and we marched there section by section. Outside we were ordered "Fall out for church". The wireless mechanics did not budge, and the order was repeated by a Sergeant Major who had left the shed to see what the matter was. He went to fetch the padre, who also wanted to know what was wrong. We told him we couldn't join them in celebrating the end of the war because we were still working as hard as ever. We were excused from the service and we went back to work. However, within a couple of hours, a large staff car with two senior officers arrived and took Colonel Whiteley away to HQ. What the outcome of that meeting was I'm not sure but, after returning, a lorry took us to the beach at Grado, where we had to fit a new engine to a boat. There were also several **DR** motorbikes to ride and, with our own bulldozer, we were able to make a sort of speedway track in a nearby field. So a great deal of fun was had there!

11

Homeward Bound

OUR MAIN THOUGHTS at this time were when would we be going home. The Government had drawn up a complicated demobilization scheme which involved age, time of service etc. I was in Group 26 for demob, yet nobody knew when any of the groups would be released. The Army's demob code was Python and before that a scheme called Leave In Advance of Python (LIAP) was in operation, which meant a month's home leave for those who were not to be demobbed until 1946. That included me. Only a few members of the Eighth Army could go home at a time, perhaps two or three men each week during the summer of 1945. Once allocation was received, all names went into a hat for a draw. Believe me, the National Lottery was nothing compared to this weekly draw excitement!

I was the lucky one in August and I was told to go by train to Milan, then through the Simplon Tunnel to Switzerland and then across France to Calais, cross the English Channel to Dover and then board a train to Aberystwyth.

As I was leaving my base in Italy, the first atom bomb was dropped on Japan and by the time I arrived in Milan the second one had been dropped and Japan had surrendered. The whole of Europe came to a sudden halt. There were no trains, ships or planes that day and as a result we were stuck in Milanese transit camp. But, as always, we took the opportunity to have a good look around the city. Fortunately, most of the trams were still running and we saw sights such as the La Scala opera house. The following morning transport had begun to move again and we caught a train towards Switzerland. I can always remember the guard coming onto the train with a caged canary to test for gas in the carriages. Simplon was then the longest tunnel in Europe. Eventually we reached Calais and changed our currency to British money before crossing the English Channel and making for home.

My wife Lena met me off the train in Aberystwyth and we went to Salem immediately. I had not seen my mother or Lena for three and a half years. There was a huge welcome, as one can imagine, and, as was the custom in those days, a welcome home concert at my old school in Trefeurig a few nights later. Beattie, my sister, was also in Salem at the time, waiting for her husband Jock to be demobbed from the Navy.

There weren't many cars running about in those days either, so we did what was customary in those days – we all walked over Banc Tyngelli to the concert in the school. It was great to meet old friends, to hear about those sadly who had not returned, and who was still a PoW. Salem was very much the same, apart from new people who'd moved in here and there. By now, the evacuees had all gone home.

Towards the end of my month's leave, an order came for me to report back to Dover and return to Italy. It was now September 1945 and I arrived at Dover and was transported to a Calais transit camp where, the following morning, we were transported by lorry for five days through Luxemburg, Germany and Austria, stopping every night at a pre-arranged transit camp. It was not a very comfortable journey, but we saw a lot of the devastation that our air raids had inflicted on towns and villages along the way. I can still remember passing through the German town of Ulm, which had been literally flattened. Austria, or what we saw of it from the back of the truck, was very beautiful though colder than Italy. (I had seen a little of it before going on leave, as my friend Reg Simms and I had hitchhiked our way over the border from Italy to a little town called Villach.) Having traversed an Alpine pass in the lorry, we ended up in Udine and were dispersed to our various units.

Soon after my return to Europe it became obvious that our workshop trucks would be disposed of before our units were disbanded. Our Fiat converted bus, used as a diesel service truck, was still with us from the North Africa Campaign. But one night, however, it disappeared! We all knew that no-one had driven it out, as its silencer was enough to waken the dead. An amateur Sherlock Holmes got busy and, sure enough, there were horseshoe imprints in the soft soil where it had once stood. And we never saw it again, either.

The Army now formed a unit made up of German PoWs whose job it was to collect and disperse a lot of equipment used by the Eighth Army. It was not a nice feeling seeing the old enemy driving our trucks away, but, strangely, it amused us all at same when they took away the Leyland Retrievers – all of which had a good engine but a dreadful gearbox and no synchromesh – and so took some getting used to. Hearing the Germans playing 'Annie Laurie' on those gearboxes while passing us on the road, with their drivers very red in the face, was some consolation that day.

Soon we were ordered to a small barracks in Trieste itself. It was a sort of garrison duty as the Yugoslavs on the border were still fractious. Trieste, at the very top of the Adriatic and within sight of the Alps, had a very peculiar weather phenomenon every winter. It was known locally as the Bora. It was a high, icy wind which froze everything, and we saw many photographs of its devastating impact such as when it blew over tram cars. Bora was due to warm air coming up the Adriatic from the Mediterranean and then encountering a colder air mass coming over the Alps which caused violent turbulence in the locality. We found that it could be very stormy in the town of Trieste, but twenty miles further afield it would be a sunny day. This was the only place where a guard on sentry duty was also issued with an Arctic overcoat for the job – and he'd need it too!

However I was not in Trieste for long this time, as postings were coming thick and fast. In November I was posted to the

Royal Electricians and Mechanical Engineers workshops of the 26th Armoured Brigade who were stationed a few miles inland at a place called Palmanova. They were from the original First Army of the North Africa Campaign, so they hadn't had as long a course of service as us. I spent my last Christmas in the Army with them.

By early April 1946, after my final medical check up, I was on my way home for release. I travelled to Wokingham, Berkshire, to receive my demobilization suit and exit from the Army.

12

Demob and Civi Street

BY APRIL 1946, I'd served my country for over six years. Like my fellow servicemen, the release could not come too soon. We were herded at a depot in Wokingham, and issued with our demob suit, something which we'd heard so much about already. It was a fairly reasonable dark stripped grey suit, with a trilby hat, a pair of strong shoes and our old faithful Army greatcoat. The only trouble was that we all looked the same and with us all trying on our newly-issued trilby hats, we looked like a bunch of gangsters from the films of recent years.

We made our way home with the last travelling warrant that we'd have. The Yanks and the other Allied Forces stationed in the UK had also departed for home by now. There was much bomb damage to be seen as we passed through the larger cities. Few of us knew for certain what the future held for us, though our last employer from before the war was obliged by law to re-employ us as soon as we were released. That was fine in theory, but many firms no longer existed, some having been bombed out, others had ceased to exist for various reasons. The Services had kept our insurance and unemployment cards up to date during the war. They had also arranged that these cards would be stamped for another month after our release, during which time one would have been expected to have found some sort of employment.

There were two things on the mind of all of us at this time: one, of course, was to find a job and the other, a place to live. I was now a married man, expecting to start a family within the next few years, and it was important to me that I found work and a house quickly. I didn't find it too hard to get a job, though my last workplace had changed hands. The previous owner had passed away and a Welshpool firm had taken over, and ran the firm on very similar lines as a small department store. They took me on as a wireless mechanic once more.

There was plenty to keep one very busy at work. But many changes had taken place during my absence, mostly for the better. For instance, in the pre-war years the shop had remained open every night until 7 p.m., and 8 p.m. on Saturdays, and even then we were lucky to get away by half past eight. (The previous owner would look up and down the street for any sign of more potential customers before finally locking the door!) The first thing, therefore, I noticed after the war was that all of the shops would lock their doors at 5.30 p.m., and our shop was no different. The half-day on a Wednesday remained though. ·

Goods in those first few years after the war were in very short supply. Food and clothing were still rationed and other everyday goods were scarce by not being available except by some miniscule allocation, perhaps once a month from some friendly supplier. So, the old under the counter, wink and a nod system applied for a number of years after the end of hostilities.

Transport also saw a great change. The faithful carrier bike was the mainstay for transporting goods from shops before the war. Each and every shop had one and also a 'slave' to ride it in all weathers – distance, within reason, being no object. Bikes came in all shapes and sizes. The one in our shop had a deep basket and a small front wheel. Many a highly-polished radio were transported in those bikes, from Penparcau, Llanbadarn and Pen yr Angor even, for workshop repairs and return. However in the new post-war world, Humphrey Jones

& Son – the name of the present owners, had a Morris 8 van and, having been issued with a driving licence before leaving the Army, I was allowed to drive it at certain times for my work, though petrol was rationed for quite a while yet.

And there were other notable differences in passenger transport. Whereas before the war John Morgan & Sons ran the bus to Aberystwyth about three days a week: Monday, Thursday and Saturday evenings – with the first morning bus leaving Penrhyn-coch at 10 a.m. being no use to workers. However, after the war, the service was daily and the first bus left with workers at 8.30 each morning. Whether this revolution had come about as a result of the pressure of the multitude of evacuees during the war I'm not sure. However, it was very convenient and there was now also a school bus service running for secondary school pupils. Yes, the war had brought about a lot of changes and I often wondered how different my life might have been had I had the chance to attend Ardwyn School by bus each day.

In the spring of 1946 my parents-in-law scraped together enough money to buy a slightly bigger terraced house – three bedrooms instead of their existing two-bedroom house, across the street from where they lived. They offered Owen, who had married my sister-in-law, and were expecting a baby before the end of the year, and Lena and I, very unselfishly, a share in their new house as soon as it was ready. Quite a lot had to be done to it, such as installing electricity and redecoration. It had no bathroom, only an outside toilet but, what we didn't have we couldn't miss. We all worked very hard that spring. By the end of May we were able to move in and on 13 June my son Brian was born at the County Maternity Hospital, Aberystwyth.

Now, as then, a young mother had to find a way of transporting her new offspring around. In those days a fashionable way was in a large ornate pram, such as a Silver Cross. During June that year, two prams was allocated to the shop I worked at and, as a member of staff, I had first choice of either. I remember pushing both up the steep hill to see which one was best. The choice was quite easy as one pram could not go through the narrow passage between the terrace houses. Its appearance was rather utilitarian but it did the job intended for my family.

Back to Salem and Penrhyn-coch

ABERYSTWYTH BOROUGH COUNCIL was one of the leading local authorities in Wales for building council houses pre-war, but for the first few years immediately after the war, it was slow to do likewise, despite many public protest meetings.

We tried very hard to find somewhere else to live, as it was congested in the house. We took to living with my mother in Salem for a few days now and again, with me travelling back and forth by bus to work daily. The logistics of all this were not easy, as Salem was a few years off having mains electricity supply and there was no running water either. It brought it home just how difficult it had been for families to manage down the generations.

Relief appeared from an unusual source. The water supply to Aberystwyth had become an increasing problem with the great influx of evacuees and Service personnel to the town. Old water pipes to the source of the supply at Llyn Llygad Rheidol at the side of Pumlumon were also in need of replacement. After the war it was decided to tap into the Rural District Council's supply at Bow Street which came from Craig y Pistyll. The Rural District Council also extended pipes to Penrhyn-coch which had had a poor water supply for many years as well. Later, the Rural District Council started to build its own council houses in various villages in their area too and very soon plans were drawn for a small estate of some eighteen houses at Penrhyn-coch. I put our names down for a house quickly and we stood a good chance apparently, as I was a local ex-serviceman with two young children by now.

All such applications involved a personal interview with the local district councillor, John Thomas, Trawsnant. He lived in a smallholding at the top of Cwmerfyn some seven or eight miles from Aberystwyth. As there were no buses or any other means of transport up there, I had to use my bike. So, one dark October evening, I made the tiring journey there and back, having had a good welcome from John Thomas and the promise of a house. He knew me and my family well. His niece had taught me in the infants' class at school.

Eventually we were allocated a house. Lena and I had prudently saved our marriage allowances during our years of military service. That, together with our demobilization gratuity, was sufficient to at least get a household together. Things were still very scarce but, on inspecting our house in Penrhyn-coch, we found a few things to our advantage. The house was modern, with three bedrooms and very well built. The 1930s design had two rooms downstairs with a coal fireplace in each and also in two of the bedrooms. It also had built-in wardrobes in each of the bedrooms and built-in kitchen cupboards and a saucepan cupboard. The living room was really a live-in kitchen. It contained a combination fireplace, which heated the water and had two ovens; there was also a modern bathroom and, very much to our delight, little furniture was needed to set up our new home.

Working at Humphrey Jones in Aberystwyth meant that I was entitled to a staff discount on all personal purchases also. It was now a question of getting together all the pots, pans, china, bedding and the myriad other things that one requires to set up a home. The bulk of our spending was on a table, chairs and beds, mostly at Aston's, a well-known furnishing store popular in the town at that time. As there was no electricity, we had to revert to the old Primus stove to make an early morning cup of tea. Daytime cooking would be done on the open fire or the oven in the living room. Lighting was by oil lamps which required attention to the wicks, and the ironing was done by the old flat iron heated in front of the fire. It was a simple start to raising a family but we managed quite well. It was a memorable time for me.

BRIAN DAVIES

1946–

SON

1

Maes Seilo

RHOS, PENRHYN-COCH WAS a happy place for a childhood.

The rolling hills of Cardiganshire provided me with strong roots which went deep into the rich soil of the area. It was a haven where the mystery of *cynefin*, the relationships between *Cymry cefn gwlad*, the rural Welsh, and the landscape would be allowed to penetrate the minds of the young and bind them forever to their birthplace.

Maes Seilo was a collection of eighteen post-war-built council houses, set out in pairs which faced each other across a narrow road. Above them was the lane to Brogynin, the birthplace of the Wales's equivalent of Chaucer – Dafydd ap Gwilym. The first part of the lane formed the loop of Garth Isaf and Garth Uchaf where there was a collection of old cottages and the occasional sturdy house and the local shop, owned by Englishman Reginald Holdcroft who did not speak Welsh. He gave customers credit at his grocery store, aware that the twice-weekly visit of the yellow van from a larger rival store in Bow Street, four miles down the valley could harm his business.

The village school lay a mile down the road and stood next to the church of St Ioan's. The school consisted of two classes, juniors and seniors. The juniors were run by a stout spinster whose kindness and fair discipline was a credit to her, and contrasted greatly with the crusty distance of the pipe-smoking headteacher. He had lapsed into going through the motions at his primary school before releasing his charges to the pre-comprehensive era school at Dinas, Aberystwyth. There, his protégés would spend four years before returning to the valley to work on farms or be apprentices in building, mechanics or other essential supporting services in the community. Very few managed to win a place at the other school, Ardwyn. Those who did were viewed with curiosity, for that school was a means to leave the valley. Little did they know that their roots were firmly planted in the soil and that the land already owned them.

Resplendent in our brown corduroy suits and hobnail boots, our early school days were carefree and happy. The seeds of ambition had not yet been sown and the only expectancy in life was attending the next grand tea at the vestry or school classroom. Evening concerts were also held on a stage set up at the end of the large classroom, and various contributions from the multitalented locals ranged from enthusiastic renditions of operatic favourites and the fortune-telling of my fancy-dressed father (resplendent in gypsy costume and large brass earrings) who would surprise his audience with informed insights into their recent personal frailties (this information having been gleaned during his work as a salesman). There would also be comic recitation of 'Y Gwcw' [The cuckoo] from my uncle who lived in Llandre. His Ghandi-like appearance and versatile expressive face, combined with a mischievous twinkle in his eye, was enough to ensure success on the stages of many local and national Eisteddfods.

At night when adults would be engrossed in earnest gossiping over countless cups of tea and the consumption of fruitcake, youngsters would occasionally be subjected to lessons in anatomy after stumbling across covert activity in the shrubs. Elder brothers and sisters would be caught out and we'd be sworn to secrecy.

We'd play football in the field below our house. My brother spent hours honing his skills as a goalkeeper there. Less active play would take place on wasteland at the end of the terrace where a network of paths would be made in the soil and mud and we'd drive hastily constructed vehicles. Others sought silence in the fields, woods and rivers surrounding the village.

Escape was easy in any direction. A hole in the fence at the rear of the Jones's house led to Cae Pant Drain, a field named after a farm further up the valley. The rich hedgerow led to the banks of the Stewi. Tall Ash trees were the home of carrion crow nests and within the ivy-clad Alder lay a rough twig nest of a wood pigeon, with its two white eggs.

Beyond the stream and below Tynpynfarch lay the wetland of Ffos Cwrt. Here, spring tadpoles would be collected in jam jars. The tadpole hunt often involved exploring the soft mud and excitement was heightened by the discovery of newts or unexpected dragonfly larvae. Ffos Cwrt in late spring and early summer was a riot of reeds, interspersed with the pale lilac of lady's-smock and the golden yellow of marsh marigold. The Stewi was a brown trout paradise, but they were wily and elusive to the orthodox rod fisherman. Before I began the trout tickling style of fishing, I accompanied my father who would patiently cast a wormed line into the deep pool below Ffos Cwrt. Reeling in the catch was not my father's style. So, a bite would result in a rapid back swing of his short rod and the fish would be landed several feet from the steep riverbank. Often this method detached the catch from its barb, and we would try to find it in the long grass. Fresh pan-fried white fish, accompanied with fresh potatoes and peas from the garden would be enjoyed while telling tales of the 'flying fish'.

2

Sundays and Salem

SUNDAYS WERE DIFFERENT. The old traditions still held and not much took place on that day: newspapers were read, lunch was cooked, with vegetables having been dug from the garden and prepared the night before. Children were despatched to Sunday school at the Baptist chapel vestry, to be educated in the New Testament and the importance of missionary work overseas. We sang 'Draw, draw yn China a thiroedd Japan' [Far, far in China and the lands of Japan]. After all, Williams the minister's son was doing important missionary work in the Sudan.

Lunch was followed by either relaxing in front of an open fire or a slow stroll along the honeysuckle scented lanes in search of the nests of robins, wrens or where the long-tailed tit laid her small pearl-like eggs. In late summer there would be an abundance of hazelnuts which we cracked between our teeth and their contents were consumed as a hors d'oeuvre before turning our attention to the sweet black fruit of the hedgerow briar. After an early afternoon tea, weather permitting, a further two-mile walk would be made to attend evening service at the Congregational chapel at Salem. We changed into Sunday best, with its starched collars and ties, dark suits and shining shoes – not wholly suitable for an uphill walk on a warm spring or summer afternoon. We'd walk past the shop, firmly shut for the Sabbath, and the Baptist chapel which would later play an important part in my life. At Brynhyfryd, a solid house behind which was located John Morgan's bus garage, there was a parting of the ways. The road to the right continued up to the isolated hamlet of Pen Rhiw or descended steeply to the quiet seclusion of Trefeurig or Penbontrhydybeddau – a village blessed with two names. Our journey took us left however, along the narrow road with its grass crest guiding us up the steep hill past a colonial-style bungalow with the curious name of Columbia.

On the approach to Salem hamlet a large Manse was situated, but it was no longer blessed with an incumbent minister, as the population had dwindled when the mineral mines had closed. The likes of the Reverends Llewelyn Morgan and Elias Jackson had long departed. The chapel was served by a variety of colourful part-time preachers from all over the county, and they still clung to the fire and brimstone delivery of sermons from the heyday of evangelicalism in rural Wales.

Past the Manse gate and on the right was a patch of ground surrounded on three sides by a crumbling moss-covered wall. It was owned by the first three stone-built houses, and there were deposited a mixture of kitchen waste, vegetable peelings, teapot contents, night soil urine and ash from open fires and wall ovens. This organic matter from the *tomen* would be divided in spring and added to gardens to improve the hard-worked soil.

My father was born in the first house of the terrace. My grandmother, Marged Ann Davies or Mam-gu Salem was a woman of determined manner and abrupt speech. Beside the house lay a garden entered via a narrow gate which accessed the scullery door as well. A path led directly up the slope to the top of the plot where there was a tall wooden closet, complete with a square timber seat above a galvanised steel bucket. This was the only toilet available to the household, and there was need for raincoats on inclement days. Alongside the gate was a large steel drum where water was channelled from a downpipe draining from the roof of the cottage. There was no running water in the house and water from the garden butt would be used on washing day. This rain secured water softness, economising on the quantity of soap required. Drinking water was carried from a pump located a hundred yards beyond the terrace: the Sunday supply was carried the previous day, as it was inappropriate to fetch water on the Sabbath. As our young bodies grew stronger we would help in drawing water and carrying heavy white enamel pails, covered with a muslin cloth, to the scullery.

The main room of the house was dark: cool in summer and warm in winter. Draughts were prevented by the tall back of the settle. In the far corner, on a polished table was a glass-cased Victorian *tableau vivant* of a stuffed badger in proud possession of a rabbit. Alongside stood a dresser with its fading blue crockery and small selection of lustre jugs. In the opposite corner was a small table covered with a cream cloth upon which was the family Bible – an impressive large, faded brown leather volume with a gilt clasp closure. The fireplace was open, with a large black cast kettle which supplied endless cups of tea. The black-leaded hearth and oven was cleaned daily and an assortment of strong long-handled implements were used to trim and tease the almost year-round fire into a comforting supply of heat, or an inferno on bread-baking days.

This cosy room led to the scullery, where an old linen press-style cupboard held the family's food. Large hooks protruded from the ceiling where hams and bacon were suspended after the annual slaughter of the pig. This unfortunate animal was fed and cared for by the inhabitants of the terrace, who then shared in the bountiful rewards of the butchered remains. These would sustain the family for the coming months. By the scullery door was another bucket which contained a variety of kitchen waste, to be transported to the *tomen* for composting.

A steep stairway led to an open landing bedroom which led via a panelled door to the one large bedroom. Both were unheated and the beds undulated under several covers and home-made quilts or *cartheni*. It was here that the whole family of mother, son and six daughters would intimately share cramped accommodation. Outside, the door from the scullery led to a small shed which contained coal and wood for the ever-burning fire.

Next door lived Albert Williams, an old bachelor with a friendly but serious face. He was a poet of the soil and typical of this peaceful, remote place. The last cottage was the home of an immigrant, a gentle man simply known as Field, whose retirement passion was fishing and shooting. He integrated happily and had a gamekeeper's pleasure of what the countryside offered in all its seasons. His terrace home was a quiet retreat and differed greatly from the home we sat in which was alive with the chatter and movement.

There were more cottages further along the road, neat and prim with their bright white lime-washed walls and dark painted doors and windows. They were the homes of other elderly residents. The easternmost cottage was home to a mother and her only son, Ifor, who was my father's best friend from childhood days. This frail woman sat quietly contemplating her past beside the glow of an open fire. The contents of the cottage were spartan. There was a downstairs bedroom and a half-loft bedroom which was squeezed in under the timbered roof: it was reached using a steep ladder which an elderly person could no longer negotiate.

Next door was the home of bachelor John Davy. My family respected him greatly because he looked after my father when my grandfather was forced to look for work in the south Wales coalfields. A short, stocky man with a benevolent presence. He lived simply in harmony with the tranquillity of the hamlet.

Beyond the cottages lay a solid house known as Tanffordd. Then there was the Chapel House and on the right, Penrhiw. On the other side of the lane was the village shop. The proprietor was Mr Stanley, an Englishman from the Midlands; he was yet another example of the entrepreneurial effort in this community. Two further small cottages led to another lane: on the left a sprawling wooden-constructed bungalow, the home of Mrs Kent. Opposite the bungalow was a large field containing poultry houses. A gander patrolled his territory with aggression, which would often lead to us beating a hasty retreat while accompanying mam-gu to collect eggs. Mam-gu would also occasionally sacrifice a young hen to grace the table. The last stone cottage was near a secluded track, which descended to Coedgruffydd Farm, whose local importance was reflected in the fact that the hamlet was often referred to as Salem Coedgruffydd.

Opposite the village shop, iron gates led to the chapel cemetery. When the chapel was built in the early nineteenth century the local population was large due to the mining industry – a far cry from the tiny throng who now graced this house of worship. We would be ushered in silence towards the pews on the left side. We sat down on narrow benches in the second row back from the *set fawr*, which was occupied by the deacons who scrutinised their congregation. The service would be led by a peripatetic minister and there would be brave attempts at exerting some vigour or *hwyl* into the long hymns. On leaving there would be an exchange of news and updates on the well-being of the scattered agricultural community. During longer days of late spring, summer and early autumn we'd walk slowly home and explore the hedgerows. On the shorter days of winter, or during bad weather, lifts in the black car of the local undertaker would be greatly appreciated.

Weekday visits to mam-gu would mean helping in a garden. This lay below Gwargerddi cottage, whose occupant was an elderly woman no longer able to manage cultivating it. However, she was happy that others could help out in exchange for a share of the harvest. A summer evening would often end with a walk to the tiny hamlet of Penrhiw – a row of small cottages lying within high hedges to shelter them from the strong winds which blew across the exposed ridge. A stile on the ridge gave access to a steep rough track which descended down to the neighbouring village's primary school where my father was educated. In summer we'd walk through the overpowering perfume of gorse and heather to watch throngs of wild rabbits grazing. On the hillside lay the workings of an old trial mine where mineral exploiters of the past had hoped to find wealth. These workings were now full of cold water and, in very dry summers, this would be laboriously carried up the track to Penrhiw and then down to Salem, whose supply from the pump would decline with the receding water table and not be sufficient for the needs of the community. The land provided in many ways, and those who lived there appreciated the harmony of its seasonal cycle.

3

Transport, Aberystwyth and Village Life

GETTING AROUND IN those days meant using a Bedford bus which ran from the garage at the rear of Brynhyfryd. These Bedfords were valued in the entire valley as vital arteries for travelling from village to village, and from the village to Aberystwyth.

An ancient oak stood at the end of Garth Isaf Lane. Its canopy overhung the hedge and road and provided shelter while waiting for the Bedford bus. We would take the bus with our mother to visit our grandparents, Lizzie and William Richard James, who lived at Edge Hill Road in Aberystwyth. From the back garden of their home it was possible to see the whole town laid out below. These regular visits on the bus to town boosted our confidence, especially when my brother and I finished primary education there. At other times the town visits would result in cinema treats with dad-cu Wil, who would often choose to watch a Western. There were three picture houses in Aberystwyth then: the Coliseum, Celtic and Pier. We doted on our grandfather as he was supportive, yet firm, and had an earthy honesty. He was the head gardener of the Corporation's horticultural enterprise and had an infectious interest in the soil and in its ability to give simple pleasure to people.

The seasonal changes would provide a wealth of agricultural experiences on the local farms and in the large rectangle garden at the rear of our home, Rhos. In the early spring there would be a delivery of farmyard manure which would be spread and dug in. Then my father would collect sheep droppings from the local hills. These would then be placed in a sackcloth bag in a large steel drum containing water, and decomposition would produce a rich, pungent liquid which would be drizzled onto the garden in spring. Healthy growth of vegetables such as potatoes, runner beans, peas, cabbage, broad beans, carrots, as well as succulent strawberries, raspberries, blackcurrants and gooseberries would result.

Spring was the time for preparing the soil and sowing, summer for weeding and earthing-up and late summer and early autumn was the season of plenty. The whole family would supply seasonal farm labour at Coedgruffydd Farm also. Spring involved sowing straight rows of ploughed fields. Late summer and early autumn meant hard manual labour, harvesting hay and then the picking, bagging and storing potatoes, carrots and swedes. The reward for all the hard labour at Coedgruffydd Farm was rows of produce for the family which would be collected, bagged and later transported back to Rhos for winter storage in the brick-built shed at rear of the house. These vegetables would be the basis for a winter *cawl*, a hot wholesome soup which greeted us when we arrived home from school during the dark days of winter. We enjoyed the *cawl* all the more because we'd had a hand in sowing and harvesting its contents.

In summer lawns had to be trimmed and there was the work of tending neat flowerbeds. The long evenings also provided opportunities for play, and children of would come together and their light-hearted laughter would echo across the valley. But the chatty gatherings could be escaped. The lane down to the Felin and the ford would beckon a quiet exploration of Cwm Felin. Frequent visits of the wooded valley meant that we became familiar with the variety of its inhabitants. An old tree, once struck by lightning then hollowed with age, provided homes to jackdaws and a tawny owl. A tall ivy-encrusted Beech was the home of a pair of kestrels and on the hillside the Elm trees reverberated to the raucous quarrelling of rooks. At the far end of the valley clear water flowed into the Stewi and it was overlooked by Cwm Bwa, a farm with ancient pedigree. Behind this farm lay an intricate network of footpaths through a patchwork of fields. Late summer evenings would be a good time to visit Salem and we would go via Garth Isaf, and follow the narrow lane past Tai Bach toward Brogynin. There would be a detour up to the large farmhouse of Brogynin Fawr, set on the side of the hill overlooking the lane and the river. The farm and its outbuildings were surrounded by Horse Chestnut trees and provided conkers which would be collected after throwing lengths of timber high into the canopies of the trees to dislodge the prickly green containers. These brown jewels would be treasured and taken home to be strung and provide simple entertainment in the street and during schoolyard breaks.

4

Christmas, New Year and Religion

As THE YEAR turned to a family-focused Christmas, a tree would be decorated with sparkling baubles. The living room would also be festooned with brightly coloured paper streamers. Christmas morning would herald exploring stockings which had been hung on the foot of the bed the previous evening. Other treasures Santa had left would be found in the living room: simple model farms, or a garage constructed and brightly painted by father in the shed during winter evenings. These provided hours of entertainment and imaginative play over the following months.

There would be carol singing in the valley and my brother and I would be allowed to join the jovial throng. The festive group would travel the valley and sing a selection of traditional Welsh carols by the light of a storm lantern held high so that all could read the pre-prepared song sheets.

The New Year provided an opportunity to top up the emptied pockets of Christmas time through the efforts of feet and lungs. There was a strong tradition of *Hela Calennig*, a rural Welsh ritual of wishing all a musical Happy New Year. The song or verse was carefully rehearsed and would be delivered with clear diction at each doorway, to be rewarded hopefully by coins dropped into the cloth drawstringed bag made by mothers or grandmothers especially for the occasion.

Dydd Calan cynta'r flwyddyn
Rwy'n dyfod ar eich traws
I ofyn am y geiniog
Neu glwt o fara a chaws.
O dewch i'r drws yn siriol
Heb newid dim o'ch gwedd
Cyn daw Dydd Calan nesaf
Bydd llawer yn y bedd.

The first day of this New Year
I come across your way
To ask for the penny
Or slab of bread and cheese.
Come to the door serenely
Without changing your mood
Before the next New Year comes
There'll be several in their grave.

This potentially morbid greeting would be rapidly followed with a more cheerful:

Blwyddyn Newydd dda i chi
Ac i bawb sydd yn y tŷ.

Happy New Year to you
And to all within the house.

Householders keen to perpetuate the tradition would have dropped newly-minted coins into the bags. This would be applauded by parents when their children returned home. Small groups would rise before dawn and visit as many houses as possible. They'd also know where the 'richer pickings' could be guaranteed according to the family folklore. But, like Cinderella, there was a deadline which had to be met; they had to finish their rounds by noon

Spring would herald a flurry of local weddings and another opportunity to collect money. After leaving the Baptist chapel at Horeb or the church of St Ioan's, the bride and groom would be prevented from going to their wedding breakfast by a stout rope held across the road by local children. This experience was expected and the couple would lean out and pay the ransom which permitted passage. The rope would be lowered and the convoy would be allowed on their way unhindered. The toll money would be counted and shared by those who were party to this act of highway robbery!

The Baptist Sunday school was held at the vestry in Horeb. Attendance was obligatory. The curriculum was detailed reading of the Bible. We would be expected to have memorized a verse word-perfect and this would be recited to the class. Later we would be given certificates which noted our achievements. Our teachers were a dedicated brother and sister, David and Sally Jenkins, whose Nonconformism ensured enthusiasm and pastoral care. They nurtured each child and taught us how to think.

Their teachings resulted in a minor revolution in my family. I decided to stop attending the Congregational chapel at Salem and instead joined the Baptists permanently at Horeb. This decision meant an intense indoctrination into the new system of belief and a willingness to be fully immersed in the water of the River Stewi. My family and the Baptist faithful attended the service which was led by the local minister who, on completing the address and hymn singing, boldly proceeded into the deep water and summoned each one of us in turn to a spiritual rebirth. The congregation smiled and supported from the riverbank. This solemn occasion was made memorable for me by the seriousness of the spiritual rebirth. Later I returned home to change and followed the gathering to the vestry for a welcoming tea. I received a personalised gift of a dark blue bound hymnal from my Sunday school tutor and it was final proof that a profound transition had taken place in my life.

Listening to the visiting pastors at Salem was now replaced by a more lasting relationship with the Baptist minister, Arwyn Morris, who lived within the community. I would often meet him to share a reading and occasionally exchange paperback

Western novels borrowed from my Dad-cu in Aberystwyth. A good Zane Grey yarn would provide the minister with welcome light relief from researching his Sunday sermons. This sharing of books was a secret between us and cemented our growing bond.

The seasons changed. The slow moving V-shaped squadrons of wild geese flew north in spring and south in autumn; the dark humpback porpoises and dolphins breaking the surface of a sparkling Cardigan Bay sea, swimming north in spring and south in autumn too; the shoals of mackerel driven close to shore at South Beach at Aberystwyth or Clarach. I spent clear late evenings gazing north from my bedroom window trying to catch a glimpse of the Aurora Borealis.

5

Escape and Exploration

LEAVING THE AREA was a gradual process, started by being moved from the local Penrhyn Primary School to an Aberystwyth school. My mother was due to give birth to my sister, so I lived in town with my grandparents for a while. Ysgol Gymraeg was an innovative institution which taught exclusively in the Welsh language. The first few weeks and months at Ysgol Gymraeg were challenging both because of the learning language and the fact that the school in Penrhyn, through its rustic curriculum, had left us at a distinctive disadvantage compared to the town pupils. Hywel Roberts, the enlightened head-teacher of Ysgol Gymraeg, was committed to the progress of Welsh education. He succeeded in converting my temporary stay at his school into a permanent one. This meant daily Bedford bus travel out of the valley, and thus began a widening of experiences.

Primary education in Aberystwyth enabled me pass the 11+ exam and earn the right to attend grammar school at Ardwyn. The Ardwyn experience was a door to the future and consolation to my father who lamented his denied experience of secondary school education. Overseen by the respected head-teacher A D Lewis, Ardwyn provided an academic education both scientific and classical, but also nurtured personal growth, resulting in self-confidence. We were taught geography, history, biology etc. and also map reading through active involvement with the school's Air Training Corps Squadron.

I was given a second-hand black bicycle by my parents which meant I could venture alone beyond the confines of the village. I explored the lakes at Pendam, Melindwr and Syfydrin where throngs of noisy black headed gulls nested on the island in the middle of the lake. Bike trips provided glimpses of the old mining communities of Cwmsymlog and Cwmerfyn with a choice of return routes via Pen y Rhiw, Salem or Brogynin. The bicycle also meant summer evening expeditions down through the village via Bow Street to Clarach to enjoy an evening swim and meetings with friends from school. Late arrival home beyond the agreed curfew would be explained by an "unfortunate puncture", albeit that the inner tube valve had been released a short distance from home!

I'd visit locations further afield such as Tirmynach and Parcel Canol parishes. Long walks would be undertaken alone or in the company of my brother, who'd been persuaded to be removed from his beloved football field.

Bontgoch

The curlew's cry beckons our gaze
Over Tirmynach's lapwing laden moors
Where golden gorse protects the bracken acres
And five-barred gates become our open doors;
Leading our earnest, eager exploration
To bilberry hillsides and rough heather,
An ancient trampled and grazed landscape
Where the only controlling force is the weather.

In spring, dozens of mature frogs would spawn and mate in the pond at Pen y Cefn. The ridge at Bontgoch would be a good place to hear the squealing sound of flocks of lapwings and the occasional haunting cry of the curlew. Beyond Llety Ifan Hen an old track would be followed alongside the *banc* enabling an inspection of the isolated farm at Llawr Cwm Fach. (Its occupant was a close relative of the farmer at

Coedgruffydd.) Then we'd descend to the uninhabited Llawr Cwm Fawr and up the craggy cliff path to Craig y Pistyll. This path provided informed insight into the often told family tales of Dad-cu Salem, John Davies's long treks home from the underground toil at the lead mines of Camdwr and Bwlchglas.

The Old Mine

The released rock falls
Remorselessly reverberating
Ever downward
In the narrow stone shaft
Sped by gravity
To the final splash
Of accelerated arrival
At the waterlogged level.

The Old Man is long gone
His tympanic tapping
Replaced by a still silence
Along a sinister emptiness
In what was once the site
Of mineral seeking industry.
Now the land rests
Ravaged for eternity.

On other days we took visits to Alltgoch y Mynydd and Cerrig yr Hafan where sightings of buzzard, kestrel or sparrow-hawk would justify the physical effort of getting there. Careful exploration of the old lead mines, where spoil remains indicated the perilous presence of deep shafts, would raise curiosity and questions as to how Dad-cu Salem and his peers earned their living in the past. Sometimes we'd make an excursion to the summit of Pumlymon via Disgwylfa Fawr, before the road improvements which resulted in the hydro scheme and the drowning of Nant y Moch.

Nant y Moch

The peat-black lake lies brooding still
Underneath Pumlumon hill.
Its waters deep, austere and cold
Weeping for the times of old;
Grieving for a lonely farm
Whose quiet presence did no harm.
John and Jim no longer there
To lead country few in evening prayer.
The chapel and the graveyard gone
The buried moved, each single one.
The ruins now a cold, wet sod
Where once proud stood a house of God.
Unknowing walkers pass and stare
At a lonely farmhouse – no longer there.

Nant y Moch farm and its adjoining lonely chapel – now long gone beneath the dark waters of the early 1960s constructed hydro-electric scheme – was the venue for a visit when we could borrow a car. Unannounced arrivals would result in an eager greeting from the two farmers, John and Jim James, whose isolated existence welcomed a social interruption to their normal routine. Taking tea in the dark, cosy interior of the farmhouse was insisted upon, but we'd decline an offer of food – the prospect of dining on bread and butter prepared on a table shared by the farm chickens was a little too much to bear! The farmers would reminisce about the long-departed occupants of Hyddgen, Nant y Llyn and Pantau'r Brwyn. We'd then explore the chapel and tranquil graveyard, before returning home to Penrhyn. Both farm and chapel now languish beneath the dark waters of Nant y Moch reservoir. The brothers refused alternative accommodation at Maesnant and retired to Ponterwyd.

Monuments

Pantau'r Brwyn now lies in ruins
It's crumbling stonework walls remain
To record a lonely lifestyle
Which will never be again.

The iron of once cherished bedsteads
Lie in turmoil on the floor.
Their rusting curves of rotting metal
Tell of a life we'll see no more.

The lonely beauty of the Hengwm
Once invited some to dwell
Within the valley's rugged confines
But how they lived we cannot tell.

Below Pumlumon lived the neighbours
At Banc Lluest Fawr and Nant y Llyn
Forcing from the land, a living
Without the thought of giving in.

These decaying stonework tributes
Lie as pointers from the past.
Their crumbling walls in silent vigil
Tell of a life that couldn't last.

The farms are silent and forgotten.
Their hardy tenants now lie still.
Proud hushed ruins in a landscape;
Lonesome lie 'neath Hyddgen hill.

A borrowed car would also permit another summer family excursion, this time to Borth to swim in the sea and enjoy the sandy beach. On windier days shelter would be taken in the sand dunes at Ynys Las where occasional sightings of snake and lizard added to my knowledge of local fauna. On the journey home a visit to Sal Magor, one of my father's sisters in Llandre, would happen. We'd look forward to seeing Alcwyn, our Ghandi look-alike uncle, who'd tease and torment in order to get local news from Salem out of us.

After the war it was decided that Penrhyn-coch, which was growing rapidly, should have a village hall. One shilling secured the purchase of a piece of land from Sir Lewis Pryse of Gogerddan and in 1953 a foundation stone was laid. Gradually, funds for the building increased and the community undertook the construction, using second-hand steel and timber. Weekends and summer evenings were spent helping out and my father assisted with the installation of asbestos sheet roofing to secure the construction. He also used his skills learnt during the war to do the electrical wiring for the hall. The building was completed in 1960 and new social activities such as playing snooker on a full-sized table were available to us now. There were also concerts and other social gatherings.

I continued to explore as I grew older. Rucksacks, tent, and sleeping bags would be carried by my friends and I as we made expeditions to Bugeilyn, Glaspwll and Dylife, with its historic mining legacy. Journeys were also taken further afield with ascents of Snowdon and other high peaks in Eryri.

Teenage romances blossomed, waxed and waned and created personal identity confusion at times. Relationships were conducted in the anonymity of Aberystwyth, but the lack of evening public transport home curtailed time and meant a lonely walk home from Ffynnon Caradog or Tŷ Coch. The walk past Gogerddan, through Penrhyn Isaf, and Penrhyn Canol provided an opportunity for introspection about the recent romance, as well as time to watch birds and wildlife at twilight. Travelling home on the later 10.30 p.m. bus from Aberystwyth involved observing alcohol-fuelled antics of the Saturday night revellers. The weekly indulgences of Dic Tai Bach and others would result in an inebriated, noisy but harmless bus journey to the village; they would certainly be suffering on Sunday.

My schooling had provided a myriad of invaluable positive

experiences, both academic and personal, and led me to seek higher education in Cardiff. A birthright bond with the countryside would be temporarily broken by the departure, but the roots of belonging still penetrated deep in the Ceredigion soil.

6

Career, Departure and Return

HIGHER EDUCATION PROVIDED a gateway to a career in outdoor education and opportunities to pursue a deep-seated passion for the landscape and mountains of Wales, England, Ireland and Scotland, as well as the Alpine ranges of Europe. I was also able to explore the Far East and have unforgettable experiences at the extreme ends of our planet in South Georgia, Antarctica, Svalbard and Iceland. These ongoing experiences were underpinned by being able to return to Ceredigion, where contact with the countryside of my childhood: the quiet solitude of Pumlumon, the silent wilderness of Teifi Pools and the tranquillity of Cwmystwyth, could still instigate harmony and contentment in me.

In seeking to understand our past, the present, the timeless earth, and the mystical magic of the gentle hills of Ceredigion, there is an identifiable genetic legacy which is inherent in the bloodline of the population of the countryside.

Hiraeth

My homeland is silent and peaceful.
Content to be there and just be.
Why did I leave my home valley?
What was it that caused me to flee?

I learnt many things in my village.
I knew every nest in its tree.
I followed the seasonal changes
And knew what it meant to be free.

Now I'm chained to a long-standing Hiraeth
That's forged by an internal plea,
To return to my ancient birthright
To rest in its hills and be me.

Brian Davies

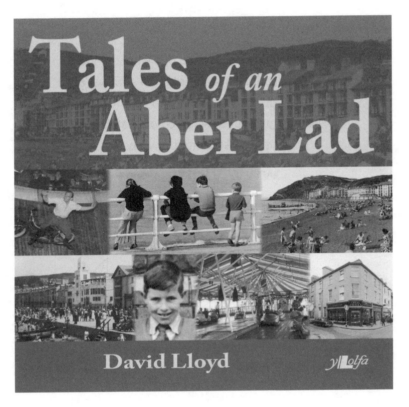

Salem Soldier is just one of a whole range
of publications from Y Lolfa. For a full list of
books currently in print, send now for your
free copy of our new full-colour catalogue.
Or simply surf into our website

www.ylolfa.com

for secure on-line ordering.

TALYBONT CEREDIGION CYMRU SY24 5HE
e-mail ylolfa@ylolfa.com
website www.ylolfa.com
phone (01970) 832 304
fax 832 782